To
Lively [illegible]
fisherfolk
in
my family —
pass this
marvy groovy
book around!

THE WHALE THAT LIT THE WORLD

Published in the United States by Lost City Press
Bolinas, California
The Whale That Lit the World
Josh Churchman
ISBN: 978-0-359-22597-2
Cover design by Jerry McKenzie
Cover photo by Kyle Churchamn
Illustrations by Josh Churchman
Last page photos by Andrew Kleinberg
Manufactured in the United States of America
FIRST EDITION

THE WHALE THAT LIT THE WORLD

by

Josh Churchman

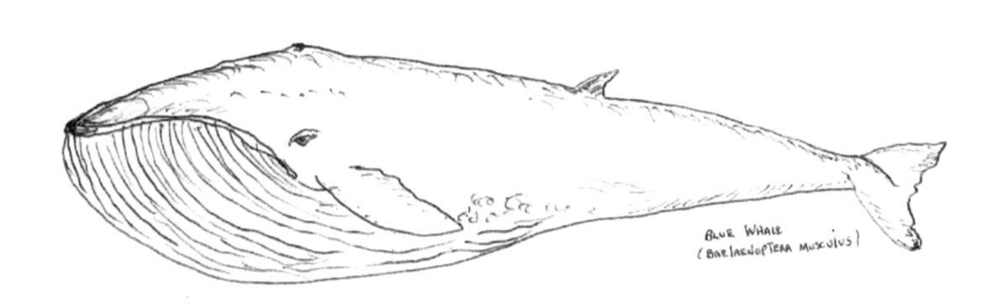

FISHING

My parents claimed I caught my first fish when I was two years old. It was on a pier, somewhere in one of the Great Lakes. I don't remember the fish, but I'll bet it was small, and I hope they made me throw it back.

Fishing and parents can both teach you a valuable lesson on how to live your life.

A few years had passed when a friend and I went fishing on a pier in San Francisco. He had been invited to spend the weekend with us, and fishing was how we had fun together.

The fishing was good that day, and we proudly came home with a dozen small fish that we plunked down on the kitchen counter where my mom was making spaghetti sauce for our dinner.

We were just leaving the kitchen to go watch TV when my mom stopped what she was doing and asked us to show her what we had caught. We gladly opened up our bag and showed her the bounty of three- and four-inch-long shiner perch we had brought home for her.

She admired our fish and made us feel like the men of the house. We had brought home the meat for dinner, and she was so proud of us. We started to leave for our afternoon TV show when she stopped us and asked if we would kindly clean the fish for her because she was too busy making the sauce for the spaghetti. Reluctantly we agreed.

Great hunters like us were supposed to bring home the dinner, but we didn't think we would have to clean it. The women of the tribe did the preparation; the hunter's job was the killing of the beast.

It turned out that three-inch fish are not that easy to clean. We each took a fish, and we each tried a different method. The scales all had to come off, and the guts obviously had to be removed, but do the heads stay on or not?

Several hours went by before the last perch was finally cleaned. The downstairs sink was a mess. We had missed our TV show, and I remember not feeling like the happy hunter who had brought the fish back to the kitchen.

The smell of the spaghetti sauce filled the air, and the pot of noodles was boiling away on the stove. My mom, Gloria, looked at the fish and with her sweetest voice praised us on what a nice job we had done cleaning them. She then looked sorry and concerned and told us that there were too few fish for all four of us to enjoy. Lucky for us she had made the spaghetti. We could have all the fish, and she and my dad would suffer through with the meager meal of spaghetti and noodles.

To her credit, she did a fine job of frying up those tiny fish, and she served them with salad and plain noodles on the side. To our surprise, she even allowed us to take our plates downstairs and watch TV while we ate. A nice reward for us being such good fishermen.

The fish were terrible. The bones had bones. Every bite had some scales mixed with the tiny bit of meat, and the aftertaste from those tiny perch was like iodine. It was the worst meal either of us had ever had. An hour later we came back upstairs with our plates still full of fish and bones. We were still hungry but reluctant to admit it.

"You didn't eat all your fish," she says. "Didn't you like them?" And slowly the truth came out. She sat us down, and we had a little talk. She had known all along how bad those fish were going to be, but she wanted to teach us an important lesson. If you are going to take something's life, you should honor it and eat it. You should never take a life for your entertainment. It was a lesson I have carried and tried to honor all my life. We could call it Gloria's Golden Rule.

***

In most forms of fishing there is going to be some "discard." You catch something you don't want in an effort to catch what you do want. Sometimes these discarded fish can be released alive, but many times they can't.

The big dilemma is how much discard is acceptable or justifiable. Discarding an unwanted fish violates Gloria's Golden Rule and is very similar to murder, when you look at it from a certain point of view.

In some forms of fishing, like shrimp trawling, it is not unusual to discard ninety percent of what comes up in the net. Out of every hundred pounds, ten pounds are nice shrimp, and the other ninety pounds are small crab and small fish that nobody will buy. The justification is that the shrimp are so valuable. We hope it is sustainable.

People commit murder for all kinds of reasons: emotion and passion gone wild, justice that needs serving, removing an obstacle that is in the way, but by far the sickest reason for murder is to do it because you enjoy it.

In a perfect world of fishing there would be no discard of dead fish or crab or anything else. It is a good goal to try to reach.

***

Years later I was faced with a conundrum and a dilemma regarding what to do with some salmon I was required by law to discard. Throwing back a dead shark is one thing and throwing back a big beautiful salmon is something else. Nothing goes to waste at the bottom of the sea, but it just didn't feel right.

I suppose there is the valid argument that both lives have an equal right to exist, and both are beautiful in their own ways, but a salmon would be eaten by anybody and nobody would eat the shark.

I was fishing with a gillnet. Salmon are not allowed on any boat using a gillnet in California. The reason for the law is complicated. Salmon can be caught in great numbers with gillnets. Entire runs of salmon were fished out of the San Francisco Bay and delta in the years following the Gold Rush. The laws that evolved to protect these runs banned all take of salmon, in the bay and out in open ocean, with any gillnet.

It was the weekend, and the beach was packed with people. The law says I must not possess the salmon, but it isn't specific as to how long I can have them on board. The law doesn't spell out where I must discard them either. I am sure a fish cop would not have agreed with my interpretation of the law on this particular day, but there was Gloria's Golden Rule to always consider.

I didn't get salmon often in my gillnet, but on this day, I must have had a dozen nice fish. I put them in the boat instead of immediately throwing them back, probably breaking or bending the law a little bit.

I knew the beach was going to be full of tourists as I came in the channel heading for the dock. I slowed down and caught the eye of one middle-aged guy with white skin that had a reddish hue. He was sitting on a towel near the water. "Want a salmon?" I said as the boat slowed to a stop. He looked around like I must be talking to someone else, so I reached down and held up a ten pounder and asked again "You want a salmon?"

What do you think happened? When I tossed that fish up on the beach, he wasn't the only tourist to jump up from their towels.

By the time the fifth fish hit the sand nobody was sitting around watching. In two minutes, all those salmon had been discarded, and I was once again in compliance with the law. Looking back at the beach, there were twelve swarms of tourists, each one surrounding a silver fish.

Months later people would stop me on the street and tell me how the salmon sharing went down. They were forced to deal with these strangers on the beach who they ended up sharing those salmon with. Somebody offered to cook it, and somebody brought the wine and salad, and how fun it all was.

I am sure I would have received a big fat fine if a warden had seen this happen, but I felt good about it because I had found a way to honor Gloria's Golden Rule in some small way. Bending one law to comfort another.

***

To this day, whenever I see a new body of water, I wonder what kind of fish might be living in it. I wonder what I could use to catch some of them. My mom taught me not to keep fish I wasn't planning to eat, but she didn't kill my love of fish or fishing.

Fishermen are a strange breed of people. It is almost like we have some kind of ancient disease. The disease is strikingly different for each individual it infects. For some it is a fresh water disease that takes a fisherman to rivers and lakes. For others, it involves an ocean.

The disease may come on suddenly, later in life, or it may be present at birth and follow the fisherman to his grave. Some people have it strong in their life, and then it just vanishes. Some people can be cured, but not very many.

Of all the diseases mankind faces in this world, it is far from the worst affliction someone could encounter. Water is most of what we are, and what is a fish if it is not all about the water? Wondering what lives in that water, and how to catch it, defines a fisherman. Turning it all into a profession is just one of the more advanced symptoms of a deeply infected individual.

People who love to fish dream of finding a really good spot and having it to themselves. Secrecy is just one of the many idiosyncrasies that go along with living with the disease. A close friend will ask you where you caught those fish, and your gut instinct will be to evade without really lying, to minimize and deflect an open, honest answer.

It has been said that ninety percent of the fish are caught by ten percent of the fishermen. I do believe that this is true. However, the ten percent is never the same ten percent year after year. Some guys get hot, and then they are not. Some people improve with age, and some do not.

People say fishing is all about luck, but luck is such an elusive creature. Bad luck is just as common as good luck.

If you are lucky enough to find an exceptional spot, you would be a fool to show it to very many people. If you discover a technique that has eluded other fishermen in the past, it would be wise to keep it close to your chest.

An older frustrated fisherman once told me "What takes years to learn takes minutes to copy." He was surrounded by other boats.

For the past thirty years I have been a very lucky fisherman. I didn't feel particularly lucky at the time, but in hindsight, I was living the "good old days" and did not recognize it for what it truly was. I had a lot of fun making money catching fish. Having fun and making money do not combine very often.

A measure of success in anyone's life could be how much fun you had getting there. Fishing is a hard way to make a living, or it can be a way to not make a living. Fishing can put you in some of the most beautiful surroundings this world has to offer, or it can put you in places that are so dangerous that you have to be lucky to survive. Fishing can put you in places, and circumstances, that few people will ever see, and you might see things while fishing that you wish you had not seen. It can be intensely fun. Without a doubt, fishing is the most expensive, engaging, "get rich quick" way I ever made money.

Some studies have listed fishing as the most dangerous job on earth. I do believe that the day you are not scared to go out into the ocean is the day you should not go out. The sea does not care if you live or die.

Be careful, trust your instincts, go home if the weather gets bad, and quit when the boat is full, even if the fish are still biting. Simple rules of survival that are so often overlooked.

It wasn't until the federal government took away several of my favorite fisheries, and access to my favorite spots, that I fully comprehended what I had previously taken for granted.

The ocean is, or was once, a public trust resource. This implies that you and I both have equal access to this resource. This is simply not true anymore. Air is the only true public trust resource that remains. We all still have an equal right to breath.

As a society, we couldn't continue with the "anybody can do whatever they want" policy. There would be no whales swimming in the sea if we hadn't had public outcry and saved them. Humanity has an obligation to try to save itself from itself. The ocean surrounding our nation is now being extensively regulated, observed, divided, and bought and sold to the highest bidder.

I had fished one of the best spots to be found in any ocean. It has so many different kinds of fish, marine mammals, and birds that each day was a new and different marine wonderland. I can now tell everybody and anybody where it is and all about it, because nobody will ever fish there again. The entire area was declared an essential fish habitat (EFH) in 2012, and all forms of fishing are currently banned.

One side of me agrees with the new law. If there ever was a place to protect and preserve for future generations, it would be places like the Cordell Bank.

***

This poses another question along with another dilemma. The question is, how do we protect a fish and still continue to harvest it? How do we create sustainability? The dilemma is that there is no answer that doesn't have some negative consequence.

"Nature always sides with the unforeseen contingency," or so the saying goes.

Limiting the number of fishermen is an obvious solution to overfishing, but how do you do it? The first attempt by our federal and state ocean managers, led by the Department of Commerce, was issuing permits to the fishermen who had catch history. We went from "open access" to "limited entry" in the first attempt to stop overfishing and protect this public trust resource.

This new system created a new and exclusive group of fishermen who had been in the business long enough to have been chosen, or who "qualified," for one of the many new permits the government had created. Every new permit, of course, had a price.

They issued salmon permits, crab permits, cod permits, net permits, and every other kind of permit they could think of. I started collecting them like people collect rare art. I could only collect the ones I qualified for, but I wanted some of the other ones, too.

If you issue a permit, how much will it cost? Or, more importantly, how much is it worth? Fishermen will get old, and new fishermen will be needed to replace the old ones. Do the old ones get to sell their permits? Or, in another way, do the original permit holders actually control the exclusive right to fish? If so, how much is that worth?

***

"In everything is everything"

Back in the fifth century B.C. a Greek physicist, Anaxagoras, said that no matter how far we break down an object, or a problem, into parts and subparts, the resulting pieces of reality still contain everything. In modern terms, I think he was saying that everything is interconnected. The ocean surely fits well with this principal.

He did add one confusing variable. Not everything has a "rational principal." When he said, "Within every problem is to be found all other problems, except the rational principal," I think he was referring to the ethical issues: right or wrong, the justifiable or the unjustifiable aspects of the problem.

***

I got my salmon permit, two crab permits, and two different cod permits without much trouble. I decided I wanted a herring permit. I thought I wanted a herring permit because it looked like easy and romantic fishing for a week in the San Francisco Bay.

I wanted one until I discovered, first hand, that William Shakespeare had been amazingly accurate when he said that "the wanting is often greater than the having."

If I could have anticipated the future, I could have had a herring permit simply by asking for one. Herring were selling for forty dollars a ton to the rendering plants, and I couldn't see why I would ever fish for herring.

Then the Japanese economy bloomed and they wanted herring roe on their sushi. Overnight herring was worth two thousand dollars a ton. The guys who knew what they were doing got rich quick.

Guys like me, who wanted a way in, had to earn points. In order to even buy a herring permit, you first had to accumulate twenty points. You got one point a year for every year you had purchased a commercial fishing license, for a maximum of ten points. Then they gave you five additional points for the first year you worked as a deck hand in the fishery, three more points for the second year you worked the deck, and finally two more for your third year, for a total of ten more points. Once you got your points all you had to do was find a herring permit someone wanted to sell and find close to one hundred thousand dollars to pay for it.

Creating a limited entry system with permits attached had turned something that was free into something with great value. This complicated point accumulation system was really designed by the fishermen and sold to the managers. The fishermen who had been fishing herring for years didn't want clueless rookies messing up their program and costing them time and money.

The first ten points were not a problem. The last ten forced me to beg for a job on a herring boat. I got a job through a friend with a guy called Crazy Paul. He caught more than his share of herring every year.

I know my way around a gillnet, and that was how herring were caught. However, I was one of the clueless rookies when it came to how and where to fish for herring. In San Francisco Bay, the season starts on Sunday night at sundown and ends Friday at noon. This law was probably set up to protect the weekend recreational sail boat folks from contending with guys like Crazy Paul.

It turns out that herring spawn in the wee hours of the morning on the smallest tidal flows. In theory, a crew should sleep in the daytime and fish all night. Some boats did this and some fished all night and all day. No fishing follows any rule all the time, so sometimes you might catch herring in the middle of the day.

My new captain never slept. We set and pulled nets from Sunday at sunset to Friday at noon. Somewhere around Wednesday or Thursday I was in a world I had never seen. I had never been without sleep for that long. I could say it was like being on drugs, but I don't know of any drug that feels like that. If there was a drug that gave the feelings I had, it would not have been very popular.

Thursday morning, we were steaming along the docks of the bay wasting time. I was on the back deck with a rare bowl of cereal. Crazy Paul came out and sat next to me. He wanted to know how I had ever called myself a fisherman, lacking even the most basic skills like I did.

I had a flash of clarity, and I realized that the money didn't matter, the herring and the points and all that stuff didn't matter. I told Paul to just drop me off on any dock anywhere and he didn't owe me a cent. No hard feelings, just let me go.

Without a word, he went back into the boat cabin and we found another place to set the nets. Nothing else was ever said. Friday noon had us unloading and Friday evening I was home. We caught forty tons of herring for the week. The boat grossed over one hundred thousand dollars. He paid me ten percent and I have my priceless memories.

I remember on one of those days, in the middle of the week, having another crusty old captain pull a gun on Crazy Paul. We were fishing near the runways of the San Francisco Airport. Paul came rushing out of the cabin with a rusty old shotgun and told the Old Italian skipper that he couldn't set his nets so close to ours. The two of them were exchanging words I could only understand half of. Paul was shouting in English, and the other guy in Italian or Portuguese. Both of them were brandishing old rusty guns.

I dove into the fish hold and stood waist deep in herring, waiting for shots to be fired. Innocent bystanders often are the ones who get hit in situations like that.

The next year I took another approach and found another kind of captain. I found someone who was in the import business and who loved boats. He had the herring permit because it gave him an excuse to have a really nice boat and write it all off at the end of the year. He imported exotic stuff from Thailand and the herring money was insignificant.

We slept when we were tired. We parked the boat on Fisherman's Wharf and had fantastic meals at fancy restaurants on the bay. We caught less than a ton of herring for the week and I didn't make a dime.

Three years later I had my twenty points and I no longer wanted a herring permit. Shakespeare was right.

****

For the sake of argument let's say that all these newly created permits are, in fact, for sale. What is to stop someone, or another country, or a corporation, from buying all of them up? Is it possible that in the future we could have sold all the rights to fish in all of the United States to someone who doesn't even live here?

Or, how about an environmental group with amazing amounts of money buying up all the permits and leaving them dormant? The Nature Conservancy recently bought up fifteen permits that control many hundreds of thousands of pounds of fish. They can now decide who can fish, and where, and how. This is a new model for managing fisheries, and god only knows what the unforeseen contingencies might be.

The current law states that not more than ten percent of these permits can be owned by one entity. That sounds good, but it really boils down to ten guys potentially owning the entire ocean resource that surrounds us as a nation. It is a fact that Walmart wants a seat at the table. Powerful environmental groups like Environmental Defense Fund are helping them find a seat.

Would it have turned out better if we had just let the old "law of economics" be the manager of the ocean like it has always been? When it is no longer profitable to catch a fish, people will stop fishing for that kind of fish. The fish will be depleted, but we didn't sell out to the highest bidder.

We can't just let everybody do what they want, but we can't let the few overpower the many. Another conundrum is born and hard choices with real consequences will grow from it.

****

Perhaps another method should be considered: protect the most productive areas. Close the places fish prefer and the fish will thrive. Find the most productive spots in the ocean and do not allow any fishing in those areas. What could be the flaw in that plan? This way the negatives and the positives are born equally by everybody. No limited entry and no permits are required.

Costa Rica embraced this idea fifty years ago when they set aside one quarter of the entire country, and significant sections of the ocean, for national parks. I have visited Costa Rica many times, and I have seen the dramatic difference between the ocean waters that are not protected and the parts that are. The fish seem to know where the line is. Inside the reserve is teaming with life, and outside, not so much.

The job of keeping fishermen out is constant. Patrol boats with armed guards check on visiting surfers and divers every day to make sure nobody takes anything.

Another obvious flaw is that if you close one zone, you put all the effort into the areas that remain open. The same amount of fishermen fishing in a smaller ocean.

There are human flaws that sneak in when these "special spots" are chosen. I think the areas where you live are special and should be protected. You think the areas where I live are way more special, and critical, to the survival of the species of concern. Should the best debaters, or the biggest bullshitters, end up picking the spots to protect?

If you think good science is the answer, how do you pick a "good scientist"? If you are a wealthy environmental group helping the process along, you might tend to pick the scientists who think along the lines you would like to draw. "Agenda-based" science is the wave of the future.

You certainly can't let the fishermen pick the spots. But…it is probably the fishermen who really do know what spots are the best spots. The scientist hasn't ever fished any of the spots. Fish swimming in the ocean are difficult to see or count. Do we want the scientists guessing?

I like the idea of protecting an area from everybody better than allowing one group in while keeping another one out. Not everybody agrees with me on this detail. The battles for exclusive use are fierce and often devious. Huge money is at stake.

Cordell Bank was picked as one of these special areas, and how can I argue that it isn't a candidate for full protection? I think it is the best habitat in this geographic area, and by believing this, and sharing the idea, I ended up helping to create a situation where I will never fish there again.

It is a sad example of irony. By believing in a method for protecting fisheries for future generations, I helped ban myself from the best spot I had ever found.

The thing that worries me most is: who will still be fishing when the fish stocks are finally declared rebuilt? After nearly twenty years of protection, this piece of ocean is looking better and better each year.

Ironically, the scientists who study the Cordell Bank and its fish hired me and my little boat to take them out and actually catch the fish they were studying. These are now the days I look forward to. Spending a day with a Ph.D. in ichthyology, and her grad student, chasing fish around in my favorite spot, is as good as it gets.

Nobody has fished these areas for seventeen years. The Cordell Bank is looking really healthy after all the fishermen went away.

The studies will not go on much longer, and these research days will most likely have been my last days to fish the Bank.

****

When I took them out in 2016, I told them I had been scared by the strange behavior of whales feeding around the Bank. I told them about several times when the humpback whales had "bullied" me out of an area by coming up way too close to the boat. The researchers rolled their eyes and shook their heads. They weren't scared of any whales.

When we got to the Cordell Bank and started looking for fish, they saw a whale right away. It was a humpback whale, with its tail high in the air heading down for a dive. Then there was another one, and then they were all around us. They were actively feeding in the very same spot I had chosen to start our day. "See what I mean," I say. The two women were looking around with big wide eyes and they weren't rolling them at me anymore. There might have been thirty humpback whales in our general area.

A large humpback whale came up fifty feet away and stuck its head out of the water. Eight feet out of the water, so its eye was above the surface. It did that so it could look at us eyeball to eyeball. They had never seen a whale do that before. Apparently humpbacks do this at times. It is called "skyhopping."

"They make me nervous when there are so many around," I said, and the researchers were quiet. There were more whales in this area than I had seen in forty years of going out there. It was a new conundrum. The risks of operating a small fast vessel twenty miles offshore, with so many whales coming up for air or frolicking on the surface, was new to me. If I just happened to be in the wrong place at the right time, I could very easily run over a whale. Or a whale could very easily run into me.

If I ever did hit a whale, it is very possible that the boat would flip over and the whale would be hurt. If the boat was suddenly upside down, and we somehow survived the crash, nothing would be working. Radios would be dead and life jackets would be trapped under the boat. Hypothermia sets in quickly in the fifty-degree water found at the Cordell Bank.

This new risk factor had never entered my mind. I hadn't considered death by the whim of a whale to be one of the risks I was willing to take.

These humpback whales got to my favorite spot first on this day, and they obviously wanted it to themselves. I put a line in the water and was about to send it down when another humpback surfaced right next to us, less than twenty feet away.

When I first met the humpback whale, I thought they were one of the slow, lazy whales. It turns out that there are no mentally slow whales. Whales, like humans, are neotenic animals. These animals are not guided by instinct. We both must learn complicated concepts from our parents, and we must solve problems on our own.

Are whales intelligent? Could they be capable of solving complex problems? My presence at that spot obviously annoyed them.

One definition of intelligence is the ability to perceive cause and effect. These humpbacks seemed to know that if they made a show too close to the boat, I would leave. They were correct in their assumption.

Another applicable definition of intelligence might be: "to imagine the results of a contemplated action." I am sure this group of humpbacks enjoyed some peace and quiet when we were gone. They had contemplated an action and had enjoyed a positive result.

"When an animal does something that resembles intelligence, people call it instinct. When people do something that resembles intelligence they call it intelligence….instinctively."

I pulled captain and said we were going somewhere else. The researchers didn't disagree. Humpback whales always make me nervous. They like to jump, and they slap their tails making a sound like artillery fire. They are curious, mischievous creatures, and they don't mind coming right up to boats. I felt they had bullied us out of a spot we should have been able to share.

I put my pretty hooks away and put the boat in gear and flew away. Whales have a hard time following me when I go twenty miles an hour.

We were soon in an area where I didn't see any whales. We didn't get everything the researchers wanted, but we did get hundreds of pounds of beautiful red fish for them and their various projects.

On these research trips I am not allowed, by law, to even keep a single fish to eat. The fish and the fishing are only allowed under a "collection permit" and that permit doesn't allow for human consumption. Another permit and another problem that makes sense and yet doesn't.

THE CORDELL

Cordell Bank, located fifty miles west of San Francisco, is part of an underwater mountain range that sits perched on the edge of the continental shelf. The top of the bank lies 120 feet from the surface. A mile west of that high spot, it drops off the continental shelf to six thousand feet deep. Eleven thousand years ago, the Cordell Bank was ocean front property. Sea levels have risen 340 feet since then. The Golden Gate Bridge would have been built over an immense river rather than ocean. This ancient river system may have helped carve the deep Bodega Canyon that bends around the western edge of the Cordell Bank.

Westward of the bank is also one of the largest stretches of open ocean on the globe. For over three thousand miles, there is nothing but water until you reach the Aleutian Islands near Japan.

Mysterious things live around the Cordell. It is not only fish and birds and whales and dolphins that like this spot. Drifting in a boat, with the engines off, there are shadows under the surface that can't be clearly seen. More creatures live here than any other place I have ever been. You can't see what the shadows are, but they are certainly felt in your sensory soul.

I often feel I am being watched when I fish the bank, watched by intelligent life forms that are curious about me and why I am there. I sense their demand for a certain amount of respect. I am a visitor, not a local boy.

It would be ridiculous to try to pretend that these feelings do not exist. It is as though the spot is sacred and protected by the guardians of the deep. I have seen white sharks here that rival, in size, the model they used in the movie *Jaws*. I have seen several blue whales that might have set world records for size. Eighty or one hundred feet long and weighing two hundred tons each. I saw a white sperm whale at the bank that could have been related to Moby Dick. It is the creatures I haven't seen that scare me most.

Part of me knows that there are not "mysterious creatures" that lurk in the deep waters eluding human contact. Part of me hopes there are unseen and intelligent creatures that have avoided human contact. This is another example of a dialectic born at sea. It is a big ocean, and we haven't seen all there is to see.

One thing is for sure, there are creatures out there that can and will eat you. There are whales so big that a flick of their tail would sink my little boat.

On land, we have tamed most of the wildness that was so much a part of everyday life several hundred years ago. The first white settlers in the San Francisco area had to deal with grizzly bears being everywhere. Those big bears are all gone now.

Every time I mention the idea of bringing back the grizzly bear to Marin County, I get the eye roll from all my environmental friends. They all desperately want "wilderness areas" and "healthy ecosystems" and they fight hard to get them in place. I ask them what kind of healthy or balanced ecosystem doesn't include a few top predators. They say they might be okay with a few mountain lions or coyotes, but they draw the line on the grizzly.

In the ocean, it is going the other way. In the last fifty years, we have stopped hunting the whales and started protecting them instead. The same goes with great white sharks, and all sharks to some degree; killer whales, seals and sea lions, and a host of other top predators are all protected. It is literally the wild, wild west out there; it's just hard to see it all from land.

As the protection continues, whales and seals, for example, have had a dramatic rise in population. Nature is responding the way nature often does.

Great white sharks love eating seals. These sharks were once hunted for food and trophies, but now they are fully protected, just like the seals. It is illegal to possess a white shark, and illegal to harass a seal. So nature does what she does, and white shark populations are on the rise along with the seals. Whale populations are exploding. The ocean around the bank is teeming with top predators. There are even sea monsters who vacation here from time to time.

We are willing to do in the ocean what we are not willing to do on land. What is the difference between an encounter with a grizzly bear and an encounter with a white shark? We are just another item on the menu to either one. You can't outrun a grizzly and you can't outswim a white shark.

MY FIRST REAL FISHING MONSTER

When I was a teenager, my dad bought me a boat with an outboard motor. He was a bold and brave father to do this for me. What is more scary or stressful for a parent: a sixteen-year-old driving on a freeway in a car, or a sixteen-year-old in a small boat out in the real ocean? My dad let me do both.

I think he saw how the fishing disease I had was not going away any time soon. He took a big chance sending me out on the ocean at that age. It could easily have killed me. Parents just have to let go sometimes. Children seldom do what you hope they will do. They were born to surprise their parents. That first car, a tiny boat in the big ocean, I thank my mom and dad for having faith.

It was a boat built for a lake. She was built with thin plywood that had some fiberglass as an outside layer. She would probably have been fine for many years in any place but the ocean. In less than a year, the floor of the boat wiggled with the ocean swell. I had to spread more fiberglass here and there to keep her floating.

I loved her and made many friends in that boat. Lots of cute girls thought they wanted a fishing trip out in the ocean. I had my own house by then and fishermen start their day early. If the girls wanted to go out on Saturday, they should probably have come out Friday afternoon and spent the night so we could get an early start.

Again, Shakespeare is correct: "The wanting is often greater than the having." Sadly, some of those cute girls got seasick. Seasickness is really bad. I know firsthand because I get it every once in a long while. It will not let up until you touch land or die. At least that is how it feels when you have it.

These sick friends got a trip back to the shore as soon as was possible, except if the fish were really biting. I had one friend offer a hundred dollars if I would just take her in. I said I could make that hundred in an hour of fishing like this, and she said, well, how about two hundred? I then realized how she felt, and I took her in and she kept her money. We remained friends until she died from another obsession that had nothing to do with boats or fishing.

That Shakespearian concept also applied to some of the girls in a more romantic vein. I thought I had wanted to get to know these women better. Then, when you are stuck with one of them, in a tiny boat, for hour upon hour, you really get to see another side of a person. There is nowhere else to go, and nobody else to talk to. Some of us are comfortable with long silences; some are not. Some will not allow a moment of silence.

It was in this little boat, with one of my best friends on board (who was not a girl), that I got to experience, for the first time, what it feels like when "you were so scared your knees were knocking." It was my first real sea monster sighting.

John Steinbeck once wrote, "Men really need sea monsters in their personal oceans…an ocean without its unnamed monsters would be like a completely dreamless sleep."

The guy I was with is one of the best fishermen I know. He is the one who gets the only fish on a one-fish day. We were fishing for salmon, each trolling a pretty lure on a fishing pole. We were three miles out. It was foggy and bumpy, like it so often is in the San Francisco Bay Area in the summer.

We were out with hundreds of other boats. Everybody was trying to catch a salmon. There were boats of every size and design. Salmon are fickle feeders, and they have soft mouths that allow them to get off a hook easily. We were right in there with the smallest, funkiest boats out on the ocean that day.

Salmon are a delicacy to mankind, and salmon are a preferred food for everything from killer whales to harbor seals. The trouble is…a salmon is a hard thing to catch. They are faster than a seal, and they can out maneuver any killer whale in a one on one.

For me, they are hard to catch because they are not easily fooled by a pretty lure with a hook dangling from it. Hours of fishing may only get you one bite from a salmon. It may also get you nothing.

Salmon are one of the most beautiful fish I have ever seen. The sides are silver but the backs can be like polished turquoise or metallic purple or Aegean blue, depending on how the light is and what color the ocean is on that particular day. If you are lucky enough to hook one, your luck needs to hold on, because salmon are famous for getting away. They jump, they roll, and they can swim backward.

When a salmon is on a hook, it is much easier for other creatures to catch it. Sea lions are notorious for stealing a poor fisherman's salmon, then eating it right in front of them. I love seals, until they rip me off for a fish. Go catch your own, on your own, I say.

****

After hours of boredom, I finally hooked a salmon. It felt like a big one. An hour after hooking the fish, we still had not seen it, and the size of the fish swelled in our imagination.

A typical battle with a twenty-pound salmon could take a half hour. They swim off and turn and twist like no other fish. A forty-pound salmon is a huge salmon for this area. It is considered a "trophy fish" and it might take an hour to tire out a fish that size.

We had never battled a fish as long as we had this one. We saw it swim by a few times after the first hour. It was a beautiful coppery silver color, and the tail was huge. It was the biggest salmon either of us had ever seen. We had only dreamed of catching a salmon this big.

Another half hour went by, and finally the fish was directly under the boat, only a few yards away, and my expert friend was waiting at the rail with the net to scoop it up.

On the rod, I felt what I thought was the fish shaking its head, and then up it came. Up and up and there it was. The net went down, and the head of the fish was in it. My friend swung the fish into the boat, but there was only a huge salmon head staring back at us. The water around the entire boat was red with the salmon's blood.

There was a brief moment of pause and confusion while we wondered what had happened to our fish. I looked down and saw the whale just inches under the boat. I told my friend to hold on to something, thinking the whale was surfacing and we were going to slide off its back.

The whale never moved. It just stayed there under the boat, motionless, as if it was waiting for something. The width of the whale was greater than the width of our boat.

Neither of us said a word, but reality had slowly seeped into our souls, and we both slid silently to the floor of the boat and hid from view. We were looking at each other with great big eyes, because we knew that there wasn't a whale under the boat. It was a giant great white shark that had eaten our giant salmon, and it was, in fact, waiting for something. It obviously wanted the second bite of its salmon.

If that shark had put its nose over the rail of my boat looking for the rest of that fish, we would have capsized. I slowly inched my way to the back of the boat to lower the outboard motor and fly away, but the shark's back was so close to the bottom of the boat that the motor would have bumped it if I put it down. No way was I going to annoy this creature by bumping it.

Time went by in slow motion. There were hundreds of other boats around, but we felt all alone. Peeking over the side a few minutes later, I saw water instead of animal, and I started the motor and we flew home as fast as that boat would go.

When I got to the dock, I could not control my knees. They were shaking like leaves in the wind.

The head alone of that big salmon weighed seventeen pounds. It may have been the biggest salmon I almost ever caught and ever will catch.

How big was the shark? The biggest white shark ever caught was twenty-one feet long and weighed six thousand pounds. I'll bet there are bigger ones swimming around. Why wouldn't there be? I think the shark under the boat was bigger than the boat. The boat was seventeen feet.

It turns out that sea monsters come in a great variety of shapes and forms. I believe many of them discovered the Cordell Bank long before I did. They like it there. Some might even call it home.

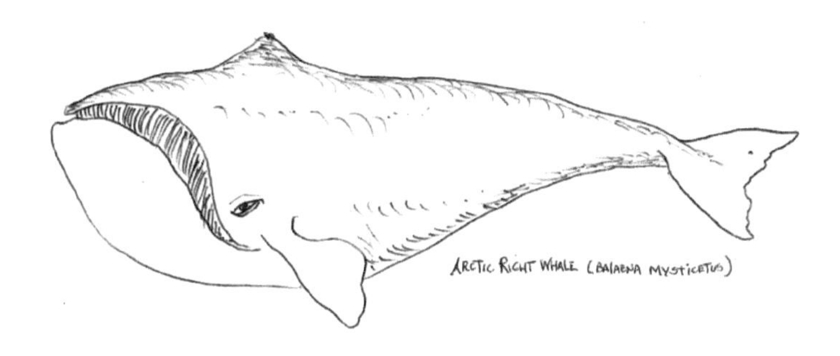

OVERFISHING....

Before the creation of the two-hundred-mile limit, and the EEZ (Exclusive Economic Zone), the Cordell Bank was exposed to intense fishing pressure. Foreign fleets from Russia and Korea were granted permits from the U.S. to fish inside the twelve-mile line. These boats towed trawl nets that were rumored to be nearly a mile wide. Back in the 1970s, hundreds of thousands of pounds of fish were harvested every day by these technologically advanced fish-catching monster boats. Hundreds of thousands of pounds of unwanted fish were discarded every day.

Nixon and Reagan sold our fish to the Russians. It was a crazy time for the fish in the sea. We thought the fish were endless. The Russians wanted a fish we didn't ever fish for, and they were willing to pay us to catch them. We encouraged our own fishermen to buy bigger boats with low-interest loans and tax breaks called "capitol construction funds." Nobody thought about overfishing. The concept and the term "overfishing" were not embraced at this time in history.

When I was a teenager, running my first little boat, I remember seeing ten Russian trawlers one day, towing their nets right off of San Francisco. All the boats were evenly spaced and staggered, one behind and inside of the next, each one towing a net. They were scooping up all the fish in a swath that was twelve miles wide. As they slowly worked their way up the California coast, Cordell Bank was in their path.

I should explain something about nets. It is a word that covers so many possibilities that people often confuse one net with another. In fishing, there are nets that tangle up the fish. These are called "gillnets," and they are put in a place that fish will pass by and the fish get tangled in them. The mesh is sized to match the head of the target fish. Salmon and herring are often caught in gillnets, but a herring net will not usually catch a salmon and a salmon net will not catch a herring.

There are hoop nets that are for scooping a fish out of the water as it passes by. These are used by fishermen on boats to land a salmon like we did, and the Indians use them to scoop fish from the rivers when they go up to spawn.

There are "purse" nets that are set to surround a school of fish and capture them in the circle. The school is surrounded and then the bottom of the net is "pursed in," capturing the entire school… sometimes. This net is used for tuna out in the open ocean, and it is commonly used in calmer waters for herring and squid and salmon and any number of other fish that tend to swim in tight schools.

Then there is the "drag net." This net is dragged across the ocean floor or towed through the water column. A typical "tow" might last several hours and cover many miles of ocean. Each method works well in certain conditions. Tuna are caught in the pursing method but are rarely caught in the drag nets. Sole and flounder are never caught in the purse net but are harvested in great numbers in the drag net. I firmly believe the drag net has caught more fish than all the other methods combined, but I could be wrong.

It is the net fishery that feeds the world. Little guys like me with a hook and a line make up the majority of the fishermen around the world, but we don't catch the volume of fish that a big net boat can. We are the "broom and dustpan" of all the techniques used to catch fish. My best years of fishing produced one hundred thousand pounds of fish. One good tow in a big drag boat could produce the same number. They can catch, in one short day, what I can catch in the best year I ever had.

Huge drag boats and I often fished side by side at the Cordell Bank. Drag netting is what the Russian trawlers were using to fish their wide swath of California's bountiful seas.

I had not been to the Cordell Bank when I saw the Russian draggers go by. I was in my teens and had just started fishing for the deep water rockfish Cordell was famous for. I had heard about it from the old-timers who all said it was like no other place on the planet.

When the two-hundred-mile limits were imposed, our own U.S. drag net boats continued to harvest the slightly less abundant fish stocks of the famous and resilient Cordell Bank. Our own government, having issued these low-interest loans, encouraged fishermen to build more and bigger boats. It also encouraged fishermen to harvest these fish as fast as they could. The catches were fabulous for a few years. In fact, the fish were so plentiful that the big-time fishermen with their big nets received as little as three cents a pound for a fish that I could sell for over two dollars a pound today.

I finally "found" the bank in the early 1980s. By the time I got there everybody said the show was over. Nobody really bothered with this spot anymore, it wasn't like it was. I had been fishing the Farallon Islands, thirty miles south east of the bank, for ten years, and the Islands really had been fished out. The bank showed me what real fishing looked like. I can't imagine it was ever better, but perhaps it was. After that first trip, I never fished anywhere else.

I spent the next twenty years looking around mapping all the rocks and drop-offs, and I still could look for another twenty. I found some pinnacles that, I like to think, no man had fished before. I fished with hooks on a line with a rod and a reel. I tied feathers and sparkly tinsel on each hook, and the fish bit them with no bait required. I would typically put sixty-five hooks on a line and fish in six hundred feet of water. We used really big fishing rods and really tough fishing reels. If you got it right, you could hook sixty large fish in sixty seconds. There were many days when we caught a ton of fish in four hours. There are very few places where two guys, with one fishing rod each, could catch that many fish in that amount of time. It doesn't get any better.

It was a dream only a few fishermen will ever see. We could drop two lines down and the fish would actually stop a four-pound weight from ever hitting the bottom. Each line could get a five-to-ten-pound fish on every hook every time. All the hooks full in one insane frenzy of fish fighting one another to get at one of those hooks. The tips of the fishing rods would be wiggling and waggling every way possible as all those big fish tried to get on a hook. All those fish fighting for a ride to the surface and a trip to the dock.

There was the slow work of bringing the fish to the surface. A boat goes down on a swell and you bring in a few feet of line. Stop as the swell lifts the boat. Reel in a bit more as it drops on the next swell. Slowly but surely, they come up. Six hundred feet is a lot of reeling, but weight is different in the water.

My boat was only comfortable with a ton of fish on deck. If we got lucky we were often home in time for dinner. We got sixty-five cents a pound. I bought my first house in California with those fine fish. It even has an ocean view.

The big boys in the big boats would tow their huge nets right next to us. I can fish around the rocks with my hooks, but the drag netters had better not. Big nets are very expensive, and the steep pinnacles of the underwater mountains that form the Cordell Bank will stop a drag boat in its tracks and destroy the net.

The net fishery crashed. The East Coast went first, with the collapse of the cod fishery. A few years later it was the same story with the West Coast. By the year 2000, every form of fishing was restricted around the Cordell Bank. Like the famous Grand Banks on the East Coast, the Cordell Bank could not sustain such intense fishing pressure. The federal government had to shut down the entire continental shelf from Canada to Mexico because fish stocks had reached critically low numbers.

Eleven thousand square miles of ocean is now protected from most forms of fishing. Hooks and nets alike are banned. This new area, the largest marine protected area in the world, is called the "Rockfish Conservation Area" (RCA) and was created to allow the depleted stocks of fish a chance to re-build.

Why did the managers of our ocean resources allow this overfishing to happen all across our nation? A paradigm shift needed to happen.

The federal government was quickly forming into another form of sea monster I had never imagined. They do their best work in the meeting rooms of hotels where neither fish nor fishermen are comfortable.

*****

Bolinas is the small town I have been lucky enough to call home for over sixty years. It is just off Highway 1, thirty miles north of San Francisco. We have a lagoon that opens out to the ocean. The trouble with having a boat in Bolinas is that you must cross a bar with breaking surf to get out of the lagoon and into the sea. Many have tried and a few have been chosen. Boats flip over in the surfs and some fishermen have died. Bolinas is a fine town to live in but a dangerous place to fish out of.

They say that Bolinas was once the home for thousands of Indians. They say it was the only place you could find a fat Indian. Life was easy here.

The story goes even farther with the myth that nobody should live in Bolinas for very long because it was not healthy to have so easy a life. I agree that an easy life may not be the healthiest life and it could result in someone getting too fat. These days all it takes to live in Bolinas is a fat pile of money.

As a teenager, I never considered selling any of the fish I caught. I gave them to all sorts of people for all kinds of reasons. A twenty-pound salmon will feed a lot of people and make those people happy and healthy and perhaps less inclined to be fat.

It was after the big oil spill in 1971 when Bolinas was changing from a red neck farm town to a hippie art community that I saw the potential for selling the fish. Two long-haired guys brought a fine old wooden row boat into town to help with cleaning up the oil. The oil company was paying incredible money for local help, and they could charge for the boat as well as their time.

When the oil money stopped flowing in, these guys didn't drift away like so many others did. They took some of their money, bought a gillnet, and rowed out through the surf to set the net every day.

I watched them with great interest as they slowly got the area wired and started bringing in all kinds of fish. I was salmon fishing almost exclusively because they were my favorite fish to catch and eat. These guys with the gillnet never caught a salmon. They caught everything else. They caught fish I didn't know ever swam in the ocean off Bolinas. In a few months, they were literally feeding the entire town with a row boat and a gillnet. In true hippie "live off the land" style, these gentlemen fed the poor and the rich and everyone else in town who loved seafood. I never knew we had halibut right on the beach, but there they were, every day, in the bottom of that row boat. The dog sharks and flounder went cheap to the poorer folks and the halibut and sturgeon went to the restaurants and the well-to-do.

Salmon fishing was still good, but I didn't catch a salmon every day I went out. These guys went every day, and they caught something every day. More on some days but never nothing.

Time went by, and their lives had changes. They moved to Hawaii and bought a bigger boat with all the money they had saved feeding the town of Bolinas. I too had a bit of the hippie in me, and I liked the idea of feeding the town with the fish that live around it. I bought a gillnet and picked up what I could from where they had left off. I bought my first outboard motor from them when they left town. Rowing out through the surf had been upgraded by modern technology: an outboard motor. The old one my dad had given me was a dinosaur compared to their newer one, and my confidence level went up with my new power.

I should probably mention the downside to the gillnetting. The ethical aspect of fishing with any net is that there will be some discard.

You should not kill what you will not use, except if there is no other way to do it? This is how I think I justified killing all the creatures I didn't use.

I often let the net "soak" for twenty-four hours. If I got a Halibut in the first few hours, the chances are that the crabs would find that fish and start to eat it. By the next morning, there could be hundreds of crabs tangled in the net and the halibut all just skin and bones. To "untangle" a crab from the net is dangerous. The two pinchers are powerful and quick. The only safe way to remove a crab is to disassemble it. I would break off the two pinchers first, then take off all the legs on one side, and out comes the crab. I "released" thousands of these one-sided crabs.

If I could only sell five sharks, but I caught fifty on my overnight soak, forty five got discarded. Some were alive, some were barely alive, and some were dead. There was the occasional bird, or seal, or fish I wasn't allowed to keep that were all discarded. I justified it all for the sake of feeding my town.

I fed the town with those gillnets for many years. Unfortunately, that is no longer possible. Gillnets were the first of many fisheries I was to lose over the years to come. Gillnets should probably be banned across the globe. If I was the manager of all the oceans of the world it would be one of my first executive orders. I loved gillnetting and I loved feeding the town with my net, but… there was a moral price to pay. I do not think it is the ethical way to feed people. These nets catch everything, and this is their blessing and their curse.

*****

The Vietnam War had just ended, and some new fishermen showed up. Refugees fleeing Vietnam had some good fishermen in their mix.

They took gillnetting to an entirely new level. I typically ran a two-hundred-fathom (1,200 feet) net. Their smallest boats ran a mile. I fished in one little area off Bolinas. They ran in groups with five or six boats in each group. There was no part of California's coastal waters they didn't fish

The boats they ran were funky and functional. The captain didn't own the boat he ran. The Dragon Lady owned all the boats. She just hired cheap labor to run them. It was our first peek into the future of fishing.

If a flock of diving birds swim by a two-hundred-fathom-long net, the chances are that twenty of these birds might get tangled in the net and drown. It doesn't happen every day, but it did happen.

When six boats show up, and each boat is using a mile of net, and that same flock of diving birds swim by, thousands of birds might get tangled and die.

This is exactly what happened right out in front of all those million-dollar houses south of San Francisco. Thousands of dead birds were washing in on their beaches.

Birds and seals and small dolphins died, and in no time the meetings started. The news broadcasts showed pictures of beaches covered with dead birds.

This new approach to gillnetting was exposing Gloria's Golden Rule to a new level. These boats provided fish to the market that everybody wanted, but it came at an environmental price that shocked the public. Within a year, all gillnets were banned in this section of California coastline.

I still believe these gillnets could be used in a sustainable way on certain species. However...considering how many gillnets are in use globally, I hope we humans find a better way to catch what we want without killing so much of what we don't want. "Nothing goes to waste in the ocean," but there is a limit to what is justifiable.

*****

It is a bad sign when scientists call you up and want to "observe" you while you fish. I was naive and very interested in marine biology, so I took them out with me when I pulled my gillnets. The information they gathered from me and other gillnetters closed the fishery. Some of the San Francisco bigshots blamed me for the shutdown.

*****

A dialectic is the art of balancing two opposing opinions. A conundrum is a confusing problem. A dilemma is a difficult choice. The ocean is full of all three for me. Gillnetting is the perfect example. It feels good to feed a town, but how much discard is too much?

Depending on what kind of fish a guy wanted to catch, the nets were often set around the rocks, and these nets would often become snagged and subsequently lost.

These nets became what were known as "ghost nets." They were called that because they would continue to catch and kill fish every day and night, but nobody ever got the fish they caught. This could potentially go on for years.

There are ghost nets hung across the rocks at Cordell Bank that I hope have been rendered benign by now. How many hundreds of thousands of pounds of fish those nets needlessly killed is a question unanswered. This is just one example of the many conundrums that face managers and fishermen every day. Globally, gillnets are very popular in the small boat fleets. They are often set around coral reefs, and ghost nets are common.

*****

If I was a gillnetter for ten years, I must have destroyed ten boats doing it. Every winter I would find another boat somewhere and fix it up only to slowly destroy it netting in the summer. I was hard on my poor boats.

When I started taking classes at U.C. Berkeley (where my dad taught), I had finally started to build a boat from scratch. It was an anomaly. Five of my friends were building boats at the same time in Bolinas, and they all thought I was out of my mind. They were building normal boats that went normal speeds and looked like every other boat on the water at that time.

My boat had been designed for the KSFO radio company as a helicopter rescue boat. It was a tunnel hull that would go fifty miles an hour over the choppy waters of San Francisco Bay. It looked so unusual that I got college credit for art calling it "marine form." The teacher never knew it was a twenty-two foot boat.

All six of us finished our boats the same year, and they all were laughing behind my back about my goofy boat. I named her the Palo. She has twin engines and is a great sea boat. She likes to go fast.

Forty years later, I am still running that boat. She and I have landed over a million pounds of fish. None of the boats my friends built lasted more than a few years.

If I had a complaint about the Palo, I would say it was the fact that whales seem to find her interesting. Perhaps it is her nice lines. It could be the noise she makes while drifting. I don't know what it is that attracts whales to this boat.

THE WHITE WHALE

"If God wanted to be a fish he would be a whale."

Whales are another conundrum that comes with another dilemma. We hunted whales so mercilessly after World War II that if the world hadn't stopped the hunting, we would have probably got the last one.

Whales have no defense against sonar and no way to avoid it. They must come up for air, and exploding harpoon guns are deadly weapons. Being big targets didn't help either.

Every species of whale ended up on the endangered species list. In 1970, the last whaling station closed in San Francisco Bay, and when I started fishing around that time, I rarely saw a whale in an entire year.

Today, in 2017, I rarely go out without seeing a whale; sometimes I see hundreds. They are making a huge comeback. It is amazing to see so many, and it is taking a toll on every other creature out there.

Whales eat a ton a day. They eat anything and everything small that swims. They can't be very selective with a mouth as big as they have. The experts say whales target krill, a small shrimp-like organism that is abundant in many oceans around the globe. The truth is that whales will eat what they can get. They will not swim away from a swarm of crab larvae or a school of tiny juvenile fish.

Thousands of whales eating a ton a day will have a negative impact on some of the other things that eat the same food, like salmon, any number of bird species, and all the various fishes that rely on abundant small sea creatures for food.

When salmon are in trouble, do you need to manage whale populations to help them? If you don't manage whale populations, what will the consequences be? How do you convince people that whale herds need thinning? First we save them and now we need to thin them out a bit. Another swimming conundrum for the next generation to study.

No easy solutions any way you look at it. We saved the whales in the 1970s with a huge public outcry. People who would never see a whale in their lifetimes wanted to save them. The only thing I am sure of is that there are way more whales now than there were twenty years ago. Hanging out with a pod of whales in a twenty-foot boat adds a new dimension to my fishing. I love seeing them, and at the same time, I am apprehensive every time I see one.

The rarest whale in our area is the sperm whale. Unlike other whales, the sperm whale has teeth. It is a hunter of large creatures. When you see a big blue whale there is one vibe, and when you see a sperm whale it is a very different vibe. Similar perhaps to the difference between seeing a cow in a field or seeing a bear in that same field. If the cow moves in your direction, you can easily move out of the way. If the bear moves in your direction, should you run, freeze, or wish you had a big gun?

Sea monsters come in all shapes and sizes. Moby Dick was a sea monster to the poor souls who hunted him and feared him. He was a sperm whale endowed with malice and forethought, and he was pure white.

The first sperm whale I ever saw was also my first white whale sighting. It was one of those "unforgettable" moments. Somehow or somewhere I had placed the existence of a white whale in the "mythical" category. Not untrue or impossible, just unlikely.

It was in the late 1970s, when my boat was still fairly new. I had been venturing farther and farther out looking for new spots to fish.

Sperm whales are not normal everyday whales. I see whales all the time in my travels to and from the Cordell Bank. I really do enjoy seeing them as they glide by, reminding me of how small I actually am. Seeing a whale up close gives a person some perspective.

Sperm whales are not seen in California very often. We get humpback, greys, and even the immense blue whales come to California in the nice fall weather. They seem to know they are safe here.

Adult male sperm whales that are not guarding a pod of females are called "rogues." The male sperm whale grows to be twice the size of the female. These rogues often venture farther north than the females. They come into the colder waters to hunt for larger, more abundant prey.

The boys grow up to swim the seas alone, leaving the comfort of the pod when they are teenagers. The females stick together in the warm waters of the tropics. They hunt together and raise their young together. The only time they need an adult male around is to breed. Their social structure is not far from the matriarchal culture of lions.

The old whaling stories of one big old rogue sperm whale trying to depose the resident male guarding his pod of females, and the battle that follows, are impressive and brutal. These whales are bigger than a humpback and smaller than a blue. They range from fifty to seventy feet long and their lifespans are similar to our own. They hunt with their version of sonar, and they have a long narrow jaw studded with huge dull teeth. Their head is shaped like a battering ram, and the blow from their blowhole slants forward at a forty-five degree angle. There is no other whale like them. I was pretty sure our white whale was one of these rogues.

It was one of those clear calm days that do not happen many times during a year of fishing. We had traveled far from shore, and we kept on going farther out because the fish would not bite our hooks in all the usual spots.

By early afternoon, we were so far out that the curve of the earth masked the land thirty miles away. We had finally reached a place we called the Buffalo Grounds. It was one of my secret spots located twelve miles west of the Farallon Islands and twenty miles short of the Cordell Bank, along the edge of the continental shelf, due west of San Francisco.

We were fishing for a fish commonly called "red snapper," but most of the kinds we catch are not red. Real red snapper live in more tropical locations. The fish we seek is a fish that likes rocks and deep water. The Buffalo Grounds area is loaded with underwater mountains and rocky terrain. It is not surprising that this whale chose this spot to hunt.

I don't know who named this remote spot, but I do know why it got its name. It is the Buffalo Grounds because it is way out west. There are thousands of good fishing spots in this area along the continental shelf of California. This particular spot was once a well-kept secret and an oasis of life on most days. This was not one of those oasis days. The fish were not in the mood to bite our hooks, no matter where we went.

There are very few places left in any of the great oceans that man has not plundered. The Buffalo Grounds are not "virgin" by any stretch of the imagination, but by virtue of its remote location and unique topography it remains one of the "secret spots" to this day. It does not appear on any chart.

If you are going to bump into something unusual in the ocean, it will probably be at a spot like the Buffalo Grounds. It may be a secret spot to mankind, but the creatures who live in the area know all about it.

On this day, and on most of the days I spend at sea, I was with my friend Kenny. We have fished together for many years, and we have seen a wide variety of marine life in our travels together. Whales and dolphins had always been a highlight for us on any trip offshore.

The whale first surfaced a mile or so to the west of us, took a few breaths of air or "blows," then disappeared. It was a white whale, and I remember feeling excited that there actually were white whales after all. We had no idea what kind of whale it was, but we agreed it had been large and it was white.

This was a lonely day for our little boat. We had not seen another vessel all day long. No other boats, no dolphins, not many fish, and no other whales; we were thirty miles from the nearest land in a homemade boat. Naturally we were elated to see the first whale, and it was a big white one. Things were looking up.

The most famous whale of all time was a white sperm whale like this one. The whale haunted the very soul of another fisherman named Captain Ahab. In the story of Moby Dick, Melville had the whale eventually sinking Ahab's ship, killing all but one, Ishmael, who lived to tell the tale. But that was just a story, and this was real.

Sperm whales live very unusual lives. They dive deeper than other whales. Almost a mile, the experts say.

They are at the head of a family of whales that include the killer whales and the dolphins. They are toothed whales; and if you believe Captain Ahab, they are very capable of malice and forethought.

The experts vary on how large modern-day sperm whales can get. but it is at least sixty feet. This whale was in that fifty- to sixty-foot range. Not as big as some of the blue whales we had seen, but bigger by far than any humpback or gray whale. We concluded that this white whale must be our first sperm whale sighting. It had found my secret spot, and we were going to have to share it.

The story of Moby Dick was based on an actual event. The whaling vessel *Essex* was rammed and sunk by a male sperm whale that was guarding his pod of females. It happened in the southern oceans a thousand miles from the nearest land in 1820.* (Heart of the Sea) The *Essex* was eighty-seven feet long, and the whale that rammed and sank it was estimated to be eighty feet. No sperm whale of that size has ever been recorded, but the whale did ram and sink the ship. It was big news in those days, because no ship had ever been attacked by a whale before. There were only two survivors.

Herman Melville, the author of *Moby Dick,* was a whaler around that time. He was a deckhand on one of the boats that went out looking for the whale that sank the Essex. One of the two survivors, Owen Chase, was given command of another whaling vessel, went back to the same area, one thousand miles off the Galapagos Islands, year after year, looking for that particular whale. Owen Chase was probably the inspiration for the character of Capitan Ahab in Melville's epic story.

Kenny and I talked about what kind of whale it might have been and I remember discussing the peculiar angle the spouts had appeared to take. Most whales blow straight up when they surface for air, but this one had a distinct forward angle to its spouts.

We were drifting with the motors off, quiet and peaceful. The view from the deck of a boat that is out past the sight of land is a bit unnerving. All directions are as one, the rolling swells being the only constant reference. The swells passing under the boat are like waves of thoughts drifting through your mind. At first you see a pattern to both the thoughts and the swell, but patterns shift, and uncertainty replaces certainty. Without a compass to guide us home, we would surely circle back upon ourselves, hopelessly lost.

Watching for whales is a game of patience. Looking out, you see nothing but sky and water when the whale is down. When they do come up for a breath, it is not for long. They blow out, then take air in, and they are gone again. You can usually tell which direction they are traveling, but that is about all you get.

A few minutes later, it resurfaced a half mile away. It was actually more tan than pure white upon closer inspection. When we first saw it, the whale was heading west south west, on its way to sunny Hawaii. Now it had changed course. Apparently, this whale had echo-located our little boat. We were the only boat in this vast expanse of the sea and somehow this whale figured out we were there. Instead of heading in the direction of Hawaii, it was now heading right for us. We were going to be checked out.

Most whales pay little attention to boats. They just swim on by, doing what they do. A dolphin, on the other hand, will come right up to any boat and check it out, often in a mood to play. A ten-foot-long playful sea creature is one thing, and a sixty footer is something else entirely. Sperm whales are not known for their playfulness or their affection for little boats. I knew nothing about any of the dangerous aspects of sperm whales at the time. If I had, I would have brought in the fishing lines and quickly moved away.

At a quarter mile Kenny and I could both agree that this was our first sperm whale. The narrow head, the wrinkled skin, the forward slant to its blow, it had all the defining characteristics that distinguish this whale from the rest. It was quite a sight to see it glowing, tannish-white under the surface of the clear blue green of the Pacific.

Kenny is a very patient man. He is tall, has dark hair and eyes, and he can fix anything anywhere at any time. We have fished together for over twenty years, and in all that time I have only seen him truly alarmed once. This was not that one time, but it was close.

At three hundred yards, it was clear that we were in this whale's way. It became vividly clear that the size of the whale had increased as the distance between us decreased. We saw that our boat was less than half the size of the whale. Interest had turned to amazement, amazement had turned to alarm. Obviously one of us had to move out of the other's way.

Banging on the side of the boat with our wooden gaffs and yelling at the whale seem like dumb things in retrospect, but so many things we do in life seem dumb when we have had time to think them over. All of this is happening faster than I can tell the story, so there was little time for reflective thinking. Both of us stood there banging on the boat and yelling at that big old white sperm whale as he advanced upon us. The whale was not impressed.

At fifty yards, I had a wave of inspiration. Start my motors and prepare for evasive action. My homemade boat is equipped with two powerful outboard motors, and it can literally jump to twenty miles an hour when we are not loaded down with fish. The problem was the fact that our fishing lines were still down and they both had fish on them, and the water was six hundred feet deep. There was no time to reel in the lines.

The thought of cutting off my rigs never even entered my mind. I don't think either of us was concerned for our safety; we were just stunned and amazed. Of all the whales over all the years, not one had ever tried to ram the boat.

At twenty yards, the size and majesty of our white whale was very impressive, and the memory has remained clear over the years. The glow of it's huge near-white body a few feet under the surface of the sea, no more than twenty yards away, was beauty with a twist.

This was a real sea monster. Everything about this whale exuded power. Fearless is an understatement. This whale had no rivals, and it knew it. One slap from this whale's tail would crush my boat and kill us both.

I put the boat in gear and moved out of its way. The whale never turned. It passed the spot where we had been just moments before and began a slow descent into the depths. The glow of its powerful body gradually diminished, and finally faded away. We never saw it again.

Would it have hit the boat if I didn't move? Who knows? We had never seen a sperm whale before, and I remember thinking to myself that one time might be enough for this particular species of whale. Sperm whales are predators of the highest order. They may be the toughest animal on earth. These whales choose to hunt giant squid for a living. They dive deep, hunting in a part of the world we humans know little about.

I had no idea there were animals like this. I guess I assumed I was the fastest and smartest predator on the water. Humility is said to be an elusive virtue, and I guess this day was a lesson. My view of my position on this planet was forever altered.

****

They say the sperm whale feeds almost exclusively on squid. In reality they feed on a variety of creatures. Modern day black cod fishermen in Alaska complain that sperm whales and killer whales have figured out how to pluck the fish off their lines as they haul them. The fish are much easier to catch when they are hooked on a line. Sea lions and seals have been taking fishermen's fish for hundreds of years. It stands to reason that a whale could figure out an easy way to get free fish as well.

The old whaling books are full of anecdotal stories of sperm whales and their odd behavior. The books are also full of tales about other famous sperm whales. Moby Dick was just one in a long line of whales with tales.

Timor Tim was a large sperm whale that had a reputation for biting, or "stoving," the rowboats used to harpoon the whales. They called a boat a "stove" when a whale crushed the hunter's boat with its tail or literally bit it in half.

Tim chose to live in the deep blue waters around the island of Timor. This whale demonstrated Captain Ahab's worst fears: a whale that is capable of deductive reasoning. A whale that is willing and able to employ malice and forethought to attain its goal. The "goal," in this case, was to have the whaling ship leave the waters he called home.

The typical whaling ship usually carried four hunting boats. When whales were sighted, two of these small boats were lowered into the sea to make chase. These boats were roughly twenty feet long and carried six men. Four men were needed to operate the oars, one to steer, and one on the bow of the boat who was ready with the harpoon.

If one boat got into trouble, there would be another to help. Two boats also upped the odds that one of you will be close to the whale when it comes up again for air. If the boats did actually kill a whale, the mother ship sailed over to them and tied it off to the hull of the bigger vessel. Whales could sink to the bottom if their lungs were punctured in the hunt.

If all four of these small hunting boats were ever destroyed or wrecked beyond repair, the three-year voyage was over. It was virtually impossible to harpoon a whale from the deck of the mother ship.

Apparently Timor Tim figured all this out on his own. He would surface near the mother ship to lure the first two boats into the water to make chase. He would stay on the surface to draw the little boats away from the big boat. He would then "sound," which means he made a dive and vanished from sight. The two boats would stop rowing and wait for Tim to surface again.

The next time these boats saw Tim was when they felt their boat was being lifted out of the water and crushed in his massive jaw. First one boat, then he hit the next. In a matter of minutes both rowboats were wrecked and the men were all in the water.

The men on the ship saw all this happening in an explosion of whitewater and in a panic they launched the other two boats to rescue the men in the first two boats. Tim destroyed one pair of rowboats and waited for another pair to come rescue the first. Four boats rowed out, and no boats came back. The ship would soon sail away, leaving Tim in peace. He was never captured.

This is a fine example of a whale using deductive reasoning. Tim saw a problem and solved it in a calculated and malicious manner. Who could blame him? This is one of the criteria used in the very specific definitions of intelligence. A definition made by man to distinguish ourselves from other animals. The ability to see a complex problem and define the various steps required to make the problem go away.

Deductive reasoning isn't common in the animal kingdom, but it surely isn't restricted to the human animal. I have seen the bird we call the albatross do it. Apparently, dolphins and sperm whales can do it as well. I suspect that the larger squid species are able to reason out a problem, but nobody can confirm or discredit this theory.

SAVING THE SEAS

I got a phone call one day asking me to sit with other fishermen and the people they called "stakeholders" to help map out the areas to potentially set aside for marine protection. The California Fish and Wildlife Department had tried to implement the new Marine Life Protection Act (MLPA), but the meetings they held up and down the coast had been very well attended and very poorly received. In Eureka, California, the police had to be called in and the meeting had to be called off.

The next year, it came to pass, the Packard Foundation was going to step in and help the state out by funding the entire MLPA implementation process. They paid for the moderators and technical staff who ran the meetings. They paid the forty scientists who would provide the data and rational supporting the concept.

The main idea was to set up a network of marine reserves all along the California coastline. They even paid the fishermen a little bit to attend the meetings. It came out, after the first few meetings, that it was going to be the fishermen who stood to lose the most in the process.

The group I ended up serving on, for the two years it took to implement the Marine Life Protection Act, was called the Emerald group. There were forty people in the panel of stakeholders, and we were separated into four working groups.

The Emerald group was very diverse. We had divers, fishermen, the guy who ran the Marine Mammal Center, and the lady in charge of the ocean division of the National Resources Defense Council (NRDC). We were all considered stakeholders.

I would have thought that a stakeholder was someone who had something at stake. A diver might lose access to a favorite dive spot if his area was set aside for protection, so he clearly had something at stake. The lady who is part of NRDC and is concerned that the process is heading in the right direction is another story. What does she have at stake?

Weeks of meetings went by and the stakeholder's task was to draw up some maps of our section of the California coast with a rough draft of what a network of MPAs (marine protected areas) might look like. The four stakeholder groups came up with four different ideas. These plans were then given to the team of forty scientists to review.

They had divided California into five districts and each would have their own set of scientists and stakeholders. The Packard Foundation was willing to invest millions into making sure this new law got put in place. I began to wonder why.

I don't remember ever hearing about private money being spent to support a government process, but I guess it happens all the time. Innocence (ignorance?) is bliss, they say.

When seals and their need for more protection came up, I got another wake up call. The guy from the Marine Mammal Center was a lawyer. I argued that seal populations were exploding in this area and that they eat four percent of their body weight a day. The lagoon where I live north of San Francisco had a historic population of around fifty seals. In recent years the population was closer to four hundred. Three thousand pounds of fish were being consumed every day from the waters around the lagoon. That was more fish than the local fishermen got in a good month. The seals were not in need of more protection. They were doing just fine.

Bob, from the Marine Mammal Center, had been trained in the art of debate. Any lawyer worth his salt can take any side of an argument and find a way to make it sound good. I was full of emotion and my passion was not my friend. He walked me around the debate like I had a nose ring.

After weeks of misery and heated debate, the forty stakeholders had four maps drawn with our plan for the network of areas to close. They couldn't be too far apart and they couldn't be too small. Bob made sure the seals were taken care of. Every place on our section of coast that seals like was on the Emerald Group map.

Many weeks had passed and I thought we were nearly done. I was ready to be done. All that remained was for the forty scientists to look at our maps.

The team of forty scientists graded us and our first set of maps like we were students in a biology class. We got a C-. We had done some good work but there was a lot of work to still be done. The areas were too small and the habitats we had chosen didn't cover all the habitats found in the region. We had neglected sandy spots and muddy spots.

I hadn't considered that I was going back to school for a two-year course in marine ecology. I thought a stakeholder was in the power position and the scientists were there to help with the fine points. How wrong I was. The stakeholder group was at the bottom of the food chain, not the top.

It took two painful years to make the final plan, and I lost access to virtually every good fishing spot I knew about by the time it was all said and done. I should have seen it coming, but I didn't. I helped them shut me down by showing them all the spots I needed to fish. They said they needed to know where I fished so they could protect me and my friends and keep us fishing. They wanted "artisanal" fishermen to have a place in this world, and they valued our contribution to local sustainable seafood.

Smiling faces sometimes tell lies. Every single spot I "needed" was eventually closed.

I did make some new friends in those two years of misery, and some of them didn't agree with me on much of anything. I made some enemies in the fishing community that I wish I didn't have. The fishermen who I thought I would enjoy at the meetings ended up being grumpy old men who weren't getting what they wanted. They were no fun at all.

The people I had the most fun with were the women who were my daughter's age, mid-thirties, who were so passionate about saving the ocean that it was infectious. We disagreed about as many things as we agreed on but that only made it more interesting. For the most part, they were well educated but hadn't seen enough of the ocean in real life. Idealists instead of realists.

When the new MLPA laws were finally in place, Marine Mammal Bob and the woman from NRDC all moved on to the next project. They are not affected by the new closed areas in any way. All of us, who still fish or dive, are living with the new laws every day.

An old wise professor once told me that "The secret of life is to look forward to what you can fail at next." This whole process of protecting special spots was a terrific failure for me and my tribe of fishermen.

I had looked forward to working on the project because I believed in the concept. We are leaving the next generation a big mess in so many areas. It would be nice to think we left them something special in a few places along the California coast.

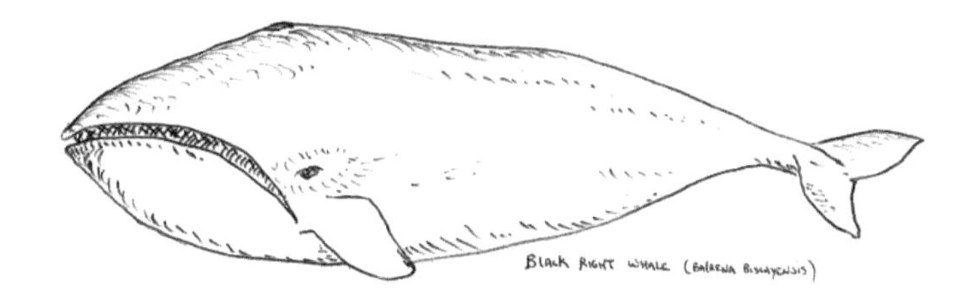

Josh Churchman

THE COMMONS

Looking at the fish mongers counter, and asking where the fish come from, tells the story. Fifteen years ago, the wholesale market where I sell most of my fish got ninety percent of their fish from local fishermen and only ten percent was imported from other countries. Today it is the reverse. I seriously doubt that even ten percent of the fish consumed in the U.S. is harvested here. We are rebuilding our stocks of fish while we encourage other countries to over harvest their own.

In this new "think globally" economy, we should be as concerned about the health of other countries oceans as well as our own. The ocean is like the air. It is one of the things common to all of us, and we all depend on it to survive. Seventy percent of the oxygen we breathe comes from the microscopic plants floating in the ocean. Common sense dictates that if we have a right to harvest the bounty the ocean provides, with that right comes a responsibility to maintain its health for ourselves and the generations that follow us.

Sadly, it seems that common sense and ethical conduct are not as popular as they could be.

In the pendulum swings of life, we as fishermen went from catching too many fish to catching too few. We went from too few regulations to too many. The numbers are difficult to pin down, but I'll bet there are twenty people employed in some form of ocean management for every single commercial fisherman in the United States.

Who is still making a living from the sea? The money is being made in the research and management sector now.

Environmental groups are in control of every aspect of fishing. The funding for these groups seems limitless.

As the ocean rebuilds, those few individuals and corporations who own quota shares and the exclusive rights to fish will make big money. They have worked carefully with environmental groups like Environmental Defense Fund, NRDC, and Nature Conservancy to push forward a plan to privatize the ocean. They put together a powerful economic plan that will change fishing communities forever.

Nature Conservancy has been buying up quota in California. They currently own fifteen of the permits that remain in the state. They have a plan.

Recreational fishermen will live long and prosper under the new plan. They have a powerful lobby and a growing population of supporters and participants.

I feel like a member of an old American Indian tribe who sees that his culture has no future. The times are changing, and there is simply no room left for small-time fishermen and the communities they live in. There was once an old saying, "The only good Indian was a dead Indian." Today it could be something like: "The only good fisherman is one who is retired and does not kill fish."

Einstein once wrote, "The reason for time is so that everything doesn't all happen at once." My favorite fisherman says "Time runs forward and backward but mainly out."

As citizens of this country, we are granted equal rights to certain resources. The air we breathe could be the last of those resources we all have equal rights to. The ocean once was a resource held in public trust for all of us to share. We all have an equal right to access, but not the right to deplete or destroy. A hundred years ago, the open forest and grazing land were also part of the "commons" and nobody owned or controlled these resources.

The tragedy of the commons is the sad fact that individuals will use these common resources to the detriment of all of us, even though they know it is not good for them or us in the long run.

Slowly but surely these "commons" we all share have become private. I doubt there is any open grazing land anywhere in this country. I doubt there is an open forest.

State and federal parks could be considered a kind of public trust commons, but government agencies tell us what we can and can't do in these parks as well as when and where we can go on these lands.

The air we breathe is still free to all of us, but we all contribute to polluting it. The rivers that flow to the sea are supposed to be part of the commons. Nobody owns the water in the river that flows through their property. It is a shared resource for all the farms and cities that exist along the river. Everybody who uses the river should be looking out for the health of that river because we share it with other citizens of this country. If I dump my garbage in the river upstream of your house, you have a right and an obligation to make me stop dumping my bad stuff in the river.

Sadly, this commons idea, and the idea of the common good, is fading away. The market wants these resources to generate money. The wealthy folks in this world convinced us that we need to limit access to all our resources. In doing so, we created a "limited-entry" system that undermines the entire concept of a common public resource. The commons, like the air we breathe, is "open access," free to everybody. How is it possible to have a limited-entry, open-access resource?

A true conundrum where there is no clear way to turn. You can't let everybody do whatever they want, and you cannot limit people without somebody coming out on top.

We have handed the job of regulating public use to the government, and there is no provision in our constitution that says the government owns these common resources or has any right to delegate their use.

Private interests like the Packard Foundation are funding government programs that they think are important. They are actively shaping how we will use these common resources in the future. Is all this heading toward the greater good for all mankind? Only time will tell.

If an oil company wants to drill for oil off the California coast, they would need a permit from the Minerals Management Agency, along with other permits, to get a lease on what is now part of a public trust. In a very real sense the government is giving away your land, or oil under your land, to the company of their choice.

Fishing rights are no different. All those fish in the ocean are as much yours as they are mine. They live in the water that is part of our shared common resource. However...if you want to catch anything in that water you will need a license, and a permit, issued by a government agency. The entire concept of "open access" is being replaced. All open access is now limited entry in every aspect of ocean management. Every creature in the sea has some permit attached to it.

Perhaps this is a necessary response to a world where there are too many people looking for too few resources. Handing out the permits by government agencies makes me uncomfortable, but who else will do a better job? My fear is that, in the end, we will leave the next generation no "commons" at all. The ocean will surely be corporate owned, just like the land. We will be leaving a legacy that tells a story of greed and power prevailing over the common good. But....what is so unusual about that. It is what it is.

Greed must just be part of the plan. A sad story that speaks to the good old days when fishermen went out and got what they got.

It is difficult to see, in the present time, that the future good old days are happening right now.

THE MONEY TAIL

The Department of Commerce is the lead agency in charge of our oceans. This concept alone should trigger some concern because the ocean is not all about the money. Richard Nixon was the man who took the oceans away from the Department of the Interior and gave them to the Department of Commerce. Rumor has it he didn't like the guy who was running the Interior Department.

The idea that money managers are doing a great job driving the "ocean protection" policies is like saying the foxes are doing a great job guarding the chicken coop. Both the foxes and the Department of Commerce are glad to do it for us.

The Commerce Department oversees the National Oceanic and Atmospheric Administration (NOAA). This vast agency is like an octopus: many arms doing many interconnected things.

Apparently, an octopus can learn to unscrew a jar with one tentacle and undo a zipper with another. However, the tentacle that knows the jar will not understand the zipper. NOAA is very similar. It has many arms all doing various things, but none of the arms communicate with the other arms very well. At times it seems like the arms dislike one another and even work to undermine or undo what another arm has worked on for years.

On one branch, NOAA has set up management councils, mine being the Pacific Fisheries Management Council (PFMC), which governs California, Oregon, Washington, and Idaho. These councils set allowable take allocations for various species of fish and delegate these quotas out to the various sectors. Trawl boats are one sector, hook and line another. Recreational groups, tribal interests, and everybody who wants a fish must convince these management councils to give them some.

Another branch of NOAA sets up and runs the marine sanctuary system. This branch of NOAA wants sustainable practices that do not destroy sensitive bottom habitats, but they are not allowed to "manage" any fisheries.

The Pacific Council gives ninety percent of all allocations of all bottom dwelling fish to the trawl fleet. At one point in history, the trawl fleet caught ninety percent of all fish landed. Therefore, they get ninety percent of all the fish in the future.

These boats drag nets across the bottom of the ocean every day they fish. They are responsible for ninety-nine point nine percent of all the damage done to the sensitive bottom habitat. The sanctuary branch of NOAA has no power to regulate the fishery that violates their primary mandate.

One tentacle works to protect and one tentacle works to maximize profit and efficiency. The longest tentacle is, of course, the arm of enforcement. These, and weather, and all the rest are funded and managed by NOAA.

***

Back in the 1970s, there was room for everybody. There were the big boats and the big boat fisheries. The biggest boats were the trawlers. They violated Gloria's Golden Rule beyond all comprehension.

These were giant boats with huge engines. They dragged nets across the ocean floor, using thousand pound steel doors to keep the net skimming the bottom of the sea. They used "rock hoppers," basically a long line of truck tires chained together, so the net could roll right over the rocky bottom.

They were scooping up every living creature. Keeping what they wanted and discarding the rest. If they only discarded half of what they caught it was a good tow. It was efficiency defined by who could catch the most in the shortest amount of time.

It wasn't even all about the money, back in the good old days, because if it was, there would not have been the seiners that scooped tons of fish up in a circular net, selling their catch for pennies a pound to be used for rendering into cat food and fertilizer. These boats made money, but it was as much about total poundage as anything else. The talk on the dock was never about how big the paycheck was. The bragging rights went to the boat with the biggest load of fish.

There were also the "artisanal" fisheries like salmon trollers. These boats used hooks on a line to catch one of the most beautiful and delicious fish on earth. When salmon became limited entry in California, two thousand salmon permits were issued.

These were the specialized boats. Most of these boats were designed for two fisheries. There was salmon in the summer months and Dungeness crab in the winter. In all the ports from Santa Barbara to the far reaches of Alaska, you can find these pretty boats. The classic "Monterey" design was one of these coastal combination vessels.

For the most part, these boats represented family-owned operations. They were the soul of many coastal communities.

San Francisco's Fishermen's Wharf, and its reputation for crab, were built by these small time fishermen in their pretty boats. The "wild-caught" salmon was also built by this same group. If there was ever a self-made sustainable fishery, it was this group of boats, and the fishermen who ran them that defined it. You will probably not catch the last fish using a hook, but you could possibly scoop up the last fish with a net.

All fishing involves some amount of discard. Even these "clean" fisheries will catch a few things they didn't want to catch. What is an acceptable or justifiable amount?

Salmon, being world famous for their cunning, would have been guaranteed a long and bright future if fishermen were their only problem. A salmon must first bite a hook before a fisherman has a chance to catch it, and salmon do not fool very easily. If and when a salmon does bite the hook, there is no guarantee that that salmon will end up in anybody's boat. The stories of the big one that got away were all too true.

Salmon need big rivers to spawn in. Any dam on any river is a gravestone for a salmon run that needs to go upstream. There is only one river in California that isn't dammed, and it isn't really a big river. California salmon are virtually all raised in hatcheries.

And finally, there were the "skiffs" like mine: tiny boats in a huge ocean using a fishing rod to catch their fish. They called us the mosquito fleet, and nobody took us very seriously. We fished for everything. I lived near San Francisco, so eventually I stumbled into Chinatown. They bought everything I could imagine people would eat and a few things un-imaginable as well.

I learned a lot about fish and people and human nature selling fish to Chinatown. It was my first bitter taste of decimation. A white man selling to the Asian community was my first problem. I could not speak any of the various dialects being spoken but I could "feel" what was probably being said. I was always the last to be helped.

I would pull up to the curb and fish would disappear from my truck when I went into the store. Then when I brought some into the store and went back to the truck, fish would disappear from the boxes in the store. They called it "chow chow." It was the small price I had to pay for delivering at their store.

The scales were questionable, and the prices were never the same two days in a row.

The typical Asian buyer is very sharp when it comes to quality. They can easily tell the difference between yesterday's fish and today's. It didn't take me long to understand the basic principal, and to see the advantage I had as a skiff fisherman. I did not spend days out at sea and then deliver my "trip." I came in every day.

If I delivered my fish the same day I caught them, the price was doubled. They didn't want to buy the white man's fish, but ...if I had a product that was not easy to find, and the eyes of the fish were so bright they looked back at you, they had to keep me happy. They taught me how to keep my fish looking beautiful. They wanted me to come back.

It was, and still is, an interesting study in human nature. It was a good learning experience for both of us.

If they treated me badly too often I would not come back. If the shop down the street started buying my fish, and taking customers away, the first shop suffers. It is a tight community in Chinatown, and there is stiff competition for the best products. The average consumer in Chinatown is as savvy as the merchants are.

WHO TO BELIEVE

The media has been selling the idea that the world's oceans are dying. They even have a date set for when there will be no more fish in any sea. According to some experts in the field, by the year 2050, unless something drastic is done, all the oceans of the world will be fished out.

It is hard to know what to believe these days. There is no doubt that some areas are in dire straits, but there are other places where some protections have done wonders. The oceans are so vast and human understanding is so limited, it is virtually impossible to know what to believe.

I do believe that if humanity were to go unchecked, we could catch the last fish. We could also dump enough garbage and effluent into the oceans to alter the oceans ecosystem in dramatic, unpredictable ways. Just like the air we all need, the oceans are vast, but are they vast enough?

Humans are putting unreasonable demands on our planet, and we should all take a closer look at how to keep our planet healthy. I hope we do, but I doubt we will.

We could become caretakers of our oceans, and they could show off their natural resilience and flourish. Some folks are working very hard to make this concept a reality. The Marine Protected Areas all along the California coast are a step in this direction.

The only constant in this universe is change, and not all changes are negative. Only time will tell what those inevitable changes will bring.

The ocean I see every day, off the California coast, is rebuilding nicely. If I were to look at it as an economist, I would say we are about to get a huge return on our investment. The eleven-thousand-square-mile "no-take" zone off California (RCA) has helped more than anything else.

The ocean is a classic example of a renewable resource. As long as the sun still shines and the wind still blows, there will be life in the sea.

THE NEW FISHERMAN

Why is it that ninety percent of all fish caught are caught by ten percent of the fishermen? This remains as one of the great mysteries surrounding the world of fishing. This rule applies to both sport fishermen and commercial, net fishermen and hook and line.

It is not just luck. Fishing is like many other business opportunities; some can see and feel where they need to be, and others spend their lives playing catch-up. The only reassuring variable in the model is that the ten percent who are successful shifts around. It is never the same guys for very long. Those who were on top last year might not ever have another good year. As time rolls by, you never know; it could be your turn to be the visionary next year.

The ocean management model has shifted and squirmed its way into a new era, away from the whole commons idea. Every important fishery in the U.S. is now operated on a quota catch share system. You either have had to qualify for a permit by demonstrating a catch history for a particular species of fish, or you have to buy one from someone who did qualify. Each permit is assigned an allocation. This way, it is possible to limit the number of fishermen and also set an accurate accountability of the number of fish caught. This kind of accurate information never existed before.

Scientists set something called the TAC, or total allowable catch, for each species and then divide that up between the various quota share owners. The commercial net boats get some, the hook and line boats, the recreational fishermen, and then we need to leave enough uncaught fish out there to sustain a fishery into the future.

The MSY, or maximum sustainable yield, is also set by a team of scientists. NOAA appoints the science teams, forms the management councils, approves the MSYs and the TACs and dole out the permits and the quotas every year based on stock assessments.

This is where the economist in me lights up. If I could just get most of the permits, I could get most of the allocation. If I had most of the allocation, I could control the price. If there was a guarantee that I had the only access to the fish and a good chance I could fill my quota any time I wanted to, I could "auction" my fish like a stockbroker selling futures in commodities. And I would never have to go out in the ocean to do it. All I need as an investor is to hire some poor guy with a boat to catch the fish for me and pay him as little as possible.

The Dragon Lady had worked all this out many years ago with her handling of the Vietnamese gillnet fleet.

This is exactly what is happening today across the entire United States. It is being sold to us as a thing called "catch shares" but it essentially puts the fish up for sale as "quota" before they are caught. It moves the whole idea of permits and "limited entry" to an entirely new level. How huge environmental groups got behind all this is a mystery to me. They must be seeing something I don't.

Whales were the first sea creature to be divided up and traded from country to country in the form of "quotas."

THE OLD FISHERMAN

What will happen to the coastal communities? They have had fishermen being part of the fabric of their community for hundreds of years. Each port is a little different, but they all need the same thing. Access to the local grounds is at the top of the list.

Fishermen need to be able to adjust to the various changes the passing years present. Healthy coastal communities need a more open-access approach, or they run the very real risk of ending up being a port without a fisherman. If no permits stay in that port because everybody eventually sold out, we could wave goodbye to the last fisherman in town.

A drive down the coast of Oregon, Washington, or California will tell the story. The boats in most of the ports are sitting idle, and the rust stains are showing. The ports with catch share boats tied up in them are still functioning to some degree, but the ports without these boats are suffering badly.

Some people want local sustainable food and fish for our communities, and some people want to maximize profits. This beautiful multibillion-dollar renewable and renewing resource is being handed to corporate America. What a surprise.

The reason our oceans came very close to being over exploited was not the fault of the many small towns along our coasts and the small time fishermen who fish local waters. It was because, in the seventies, our government gave out low-interest loans for big-time fishermen to be even bigger. We thought the oceans were infinite. Now we have come to realize that the oceans are very sensitive, and not infinite at all.

Ronald Reagan sold our fish to the Russians, and in a few short years our fisheries were in trouble. After that, the Russians showed the Americans how to really fish big.

THE OLDEST SEA MONSTER

Four hundred million years before the dinosaurs it was the squid family that ruled the seas. The chambered Nautilus, an ancestor of the modern-day squid, was the first animal to lift off the bottom of the sea and float.

This simple advancement gave the nautilus an advantage that lasted until having a shell became a disadvantage. The nautilus filled the chambers of its shell with fresh water by filtering out the salt. Fresh water is lighter than salt water and the shell could now float. As time went by fresh water was replaced by air and the nautilus developed a siphon system to jet water, allowing the nautilus to move where it wanted rather than being at the mercy of the current.

The chambered nautilus is part of a family called cephalopods. Octopus and squid are the most well-known members of this family. Unfortunately, around sixty million years ago, most of the cephalopods living in the ocean lost their shells. Creatures without shells or bones do not leave a good fossil record so we do not really know a lot about their evolution.

We do know that there are nearly four hundred species of squid and octopus. We know that the squid population in the deep ocean is large enough to support a million sperm whales who eat a ton of them a day each. We know that a member of the squid kingdom called Archeteuthis grows to nearly sixty feet because one washed up in New Zealand that was fifty seven feet long and had an eye that measured thirteen inches across.

Back in the days when sailing ships were the only way to move anything or get anywhere there was a well-known sea monster. It had names like "the Kraken" and it always had tentacles.

The ocean has been home to some fantastic sea monsters over the years. There was the ancestor to the great white shark, megalodon, who ate dinosaurs for a living. It grew to eighty feet and had rows of six-inch-long teeth. There was an ancestor to the sperm whale that was a whale eating whale. It had thirteen-inch-long teeth. Then there was the Kraken. It was responsible for pulling entire sailing ships underwater, never to be seen again. A squid or octopus so large it could pull an eighty-foot wood sailing schooner underwater.

The whale eating whale is probably extinct but the other two might still be around. Great white sharks today are often over twenty feet long and can weigh six thousand pounds. Squid could be the ones that get the biggest and they are definitely here now.

The giant squid that live in the deep ocean use light to hunt. They have cells around their eyes that can generate light. They also have cells that can receive light. They send out a beam of light and if it bounces off an object they will go over and have a look at what it is. Some experts speculate that the squid can determine size, shape and speed from the return.

Whales do a very similar thing with sound. They interpret the returning sound pulse and from that they can determine size, distance, and density. We know that both systems work quite well because these are two of the most successful species of animals on earth.

In the old days, sailing boats were forced to drift for days if there wasn't any wind. At night they would light lanterns, attracting all kinds of life up from the deep. If I were a sea monster looking for prey I would investigate an object like that.

In our modern times virtually all the boats have motors and they rarely stop to drift. Sea monsters might not be able to swim fast enough to catch them. It is possible, over the years, that sea monsters found they didn't really get much when they pulled a boat under and they simply don't bother with boats anymore.

Squid still hold the record for being the most elusive sea monster. Experts can't find adults or babies. Teams of scientists keep trying but it seems like the squid might be trying to avoid us.

If I was an intelligent sea monster I would try to avoid us too.

THE FOOD CHAIN

Cordell Bank is a very rare and special place. The constant northwest wind causes a phenomenon called upwelling. The wind blows the warmer surface water offshore and it is replaced by the colder, nutrient rich waters found in the submarine canyons that surround the bank. This creates ideal conditions for microscopic life to begin.

There are only four places on earth where upwelling occurs and they are the four richest stretches of ocean.

Life in the sea begins with the microscopic plants called phytoplankton. They are often called the green grass of the sea and they look like snowflakes under a microscope. These tiny plants provide over seventy percent of the world's oxygen. They are the beginning of the oceans food chain.

The fewer links there are in the chain the more efficient it is. If a tiny shrimp, like krill, eats the tiny plants, and a Blue whale comes along and fills its belly with tons of krill have a very efficient food chain.

If a small fish eats the krill and that small fish is eaten by a bigger fish, and then I come along, and catch that fish, and sell it to someone, the chain gets longer and less efficient.

Special spots, like the Cordell Bank, are not secret to the rarest of all sea creatures. There might be some sea monsters looking to share in the California dream. Every time I go there I expect to see a marine wildlife show, and I am seldom disappointed.

We were lucky enough to spend a day with the very rare "short tailed Albatross". They have a ten-foot wingspan, a big fat pink beak, and they are white with black tips on their wings. These were the unfortunate birds who had the perfect feathers for women's fashion in the 1800's.

They had the tragic flaw of breeding on the same islands every year. Human predation has reduced their numbers down to two hundred birds. At one point, it is believed, there were hundreds of thousands of these magnificent huge birds.

My favorite bird, of all the many birds I have known, over all the years at sea, is the Albatross. The Black-Footed Albatross in particular. These birds have a nine-foot wingspan, but the short tail dwarfed them. The black foots let the short tail have whatever fish it wanted.

The rarest whale is the Right whale. It once swam close to shore in great numbers. It is a slow swimmer and apparently it didn't tend to sink when it was killed. It was called the Right whale because it was the right whale to hunt. There are not many of these whales left.

This rare creature also knew about the Cordell Bank and we had the honor of seeing one swim by us. They have a split blow hole and their spout is two jets of air.

Everything seems to be aware of the Cordell. I can't help but wonder what lives there that I haven't seen yet. Or, what has seen me that I didn't see.

Are there sixty-foot Squid living in the deep canyons? Why wouldn't there be?

"You never know what you don't know" is an old Alaskan saying that seems to fit in regards to the mysteries that surround the Universe, and the Cordell Bank.

Humanity is just another small link in the food chain of life.

ASSUMPTIONS

I hadn't even considered the possibility that whales might have different personalities. I had assumed they were all alike. They are not alike at all. I am not sure where I had placed whales on the sliding scale of intelligent beings. I know I hadn't given them top billing.

I assumed I was the only devious and mischievous ocean-going creature. I assumed I understood who lived in the ocean and what they were, and were not, capable of.

Then there was the day the sperm whale tried to ram my boat. It was not the same feeling I had had when other big ocean going animals had accessed me at various times in years past. All the others had looked at me as part of the food chain. The sperm whale just wanted me to know who was in charge.

One day, when I was pulling a gillnet in my little seventeen-foot Boston Whaler, alone, a Steller sea lion, weighing at least a ton, lifted his head high enough out of the water to look down into my boat. It saw the fish lying on the deck, and then it gave me one of those up-and-down looks. I felt like I was on the menu, and it stirred the core of my soul. I involuntarily froze for a moment, like a bird captivated by the gaze of a snake. No animal had ever looked at me that way before, and I hope I never have one look at me like that again.

The feeling I got from the whale was not the same feeling at all. It was aggressive, but not motivated by a need to feed.

It was more like being caught in a place where you are not welcome. I had found myself in a part of the ocean where I was not supposed to be. I had blundered into the wrong neighborhood, clueless of my mistake.

I know where the whale was coming from. I too have felt very territorial about spots in the ocean I considered my own. I have infringed on other fishermen's spots a time or two and felt the same boundary crossing negativity floating across the water. But…these are distinctly human traits, emotional interpretations and reactions to unwritten law.

Whales do not live by the laws of man. However, if there ever were a being that had a right to feel territorial about the sea, it would certainly be the whale.

Why does a dolphin or a whale need a big brain? Does the bird fly because it has wings, or does it have wings because it flies? The whales evolved large brains because they needed them to survive. Acoustical interpretation of the ocean environment is complex, involving long-wave sonar for orientation and short-wave sonar for close range detail. Nature would not give them these skills needlessly.

I can understand the territorial motivations; it is the malice and forethought that surprised me. I guess I just assumed humans were the only animal capable of things like premeditated mischief. Whales, for me, hadn't possessed analytical capacity, or mischievousness, until that day.

*****

Zoologists divide whales (Cetacia) into two categories: The baleen whales (Mysticeti), and the toothed whales (Odontoceti). Zoologists also agree that all whales are descendants of mammals that lived on land. Some think these animals were otter-like, and others think they were more hippopotamus.

Sixty million years ago, right around the time the asteroid struck the earth and the dinosaurs vanished, the whales and the ancestors of the squid (Chambered nautilus) evolved in new directions. Nobody knows why, but we do know when.

One vein of thought is that whales developed sound-producing hunting techniques to locate the shells of the chambered nautilus that they preferred as food. The chambered nautilus then evolved away from shells to avoid detection from the sound beams of the whale.

*****

The sperm whale was the most valuable whale in the first great era of whaling. It has the finest and sweetest oil of all the great whales. I had assumed that sperm whale populations were way down from what they once were, but again I was wrong. The sperm whale is apparently the only great whale that is not on the threatened species list. The other great whales are the blue, the humpback, the fin, and the right. Only the sperm whale is a toothed whale; all the rest are baleen whales.

A large sperm whale today is sixty feet, but there is a jaw, in the Nantucket Whaling Museum, that measures eighteen feet. The whale that grew this jaw must have been closer to eighty feet long and probably weighed over one hundred tons. It is near impossible to imagine that this jaw was taken from the biggest sperm whale that ever lived. It is hard to believe that some random whaler harpooned and killed "the" biggest sperm whale in the sea. It could happen, but it is very unlikely.

The same principal applies to the squid. A fifty-seven footer washes in, but what are the chances that that was the biggest squid to ever live? There could easily be squid that are bigger than blue whales. We just don't know.

Sperm whales like warm water, and this too may be a sign of reasoned intelligence. The females and young males swim in equatorial waters, as far from any land as an animal can get.

It is only the large male sperm whales, the rogues, that roam to the ends of the earth. The male grows to be twice the size of the female. The big males are loaners, only joining the females for brief visits. They have swum the oceans, virtually un-challenged, for sixty million years.

All the sperm whales I have seen must have been the large males. The Cordell Bank is a cold water spot. Sea temperatures here average fifty-five degrees. It might be too chilly for the females, who like warmer waters.

Perhaps it was the arrogance, born of this dominance, that gave them their vulnerability. They feared nothing when those first men appeared with harpoons. Evolution adjusts slowly.

Female sperm whales tend to come to the aid of a wounded member of the pod. If killer whales have injured a member, the other whales will form a circle around the vulnerable one. They call it a "rosette." The heads are all pointed to the center and the tails all radiating out like spokes in a wheel.

The whalers tell of harpooning one sperm whale and having the whole pod come back to the boats to assist their troubled friend. This trait was exploited by the whalers.

The few scientists who have been observing sperm whale behavior all agree on one thing. The sperm whale is a very affectionate animal. When the big males show up, the entire pod appears happy to see him. They all come up and bump and rub and stroke with their flippers to show it.

****

Squid are the preferred diet of the sperm whale. Perhaps their oil was the finest oil because they eat primarily squid. Current estimates are that the sperm whale population consumes seventy-five million metric tons of squid from the ocean every year. Seventy-five million metric tons is very close to what is harvested annually by all human fisheries combined. These squid are consumed by the nearly one million sperm whales that are alive today. Why they prefer squid is a question nobody will ever answer. They have been enjoying them for sixty million years.

It is a good thing that we humans do not harvest the squid the whales hunt. We don't fish that deep and we don't like stuff that tastes like ammonia. If we did, we would probably have killed off the whales by now.

How these whales can successfully hunt a large squid that is both faster and more maneuverable than they are is another question. We can speculate about how they do it, and make good guesses, but truly we do not know very much about the lives of either of these two animals. How is it possible that a sperm whale can eat a ton of squid in a day, swimming at only three miles an hour? They often swim a mile down in utter darkness to catch their squid. They swallow them whole.

There is only one animal in the ocean that might grow larger than the whale. There is only one animal, other than man, that might hunt sperm whales for a living. If some species of squid grow to over one hundred feet, it is very likely that they catch whales once in a while. We don't know; there could be packs of squid that specialize in hunting whales. Squid do hunt in packs.

No man has ever successfully hunted these giant squid. We assume they only get so big, but we do not know the world of the deep ocean very well. Squid may well be the soft intelligence living out of the reach of man's hands. Or… are they the soft intelligence that knows better than to get anywhere near humanity?

THE HUMBOLDT SQUID INVASION

The Humboldt squid arrived at the Cordell Bank during a "warm water event" or "El Nino." The upwelling that brings life and cold water up from the deep and onto the bank had slowed down, and sea surface temperatures were ten degrees warmer than normal.

These warm water events are not uncommon. Some species like the warm water, and some do not. Jellyfish, sharks and surfers don't mind it at all. Other species just disappear. Salmon do not like warm water, and they will swim hundreds of miles to stay away from it.

The San Francisco Bay is in Northern California. When we get one of these El Nino years, it is like Los Angeles moves up the coast with all its masses of troublesome little fish. The south moves north, and we northerners do not enjoy the invasion.

Fish are not the only things that move north with the warm water. This time, the squid came along. They were not the real giant squid that get to be sixty feet long. These were "Humboldt Squid" (Diablo Rojo), and they were only two to six feet in length. They can weigh up to seventy pounds, and they never stop for a rest.

These particular squid have a terra cotta red color with a "clear coat" of metallic iridescence over their entire body. They have large black eyes that seem to look directly into your soul.

Until that day, I had never encountered an animal, other than a human being, capable of pulling off a practical joke. Then

I had my first meeting with a Humboldt squid. Who knows, maybe all squid have a fantastic sense of humor once you get to know them.

It was a total surprise to see the first squid of that size hanging onto my hook. We had seen the little squid called "market squid" that are commonly used for calamari. Market squid (Loligo) are less than a foot long and are the main bait we use to catch Dungeness crab in the winter months. Nobody I had ever talked to had seen a four-foot-long squid in this part of the ocean. On the first day we only got one, and that made it all the more exciting.

I didn't see any bites on my fishing rod when I sent it down, but the line was very heavy when I tried to reel it in. Kenny had nothing on his line, and it came right up. When I finally got mine to the surface, it was going straight down. Something was not right. I had sixty-five hooks on my rig, and sixty-four were empty.

As the last hook appeared from under the boat, there was a pair of big black eyes looking up at me. Those first looks were filled with curiosity: the squid wondering who I was and me wondering what it was I had caught.

There was a moment of pause. I had not seen a squid that big before and wasn't quite sure what to do. In that moment of pause, the squid had used its tentacles to grab hold of the side of the boat, but I didn't notice.

I tried to swing the squid into the boat in one swift motion, but it was stuck like a rock. It was bigger than it looked at first, so I looked away for a second to find my gaff hook to help swing it in.

When I bent over the rail to gaff the squid, I noticed it had changed positions, and we were now eyeball to eyeball. The squid's head was fully out of the water, and it seemed to have a glint in its eye.

A blast of ink and water two inches in diameter hit me in the chest. I was soaked to the bone in a second. My blue shirt was now a brownish color, and I was spluttering for air.

When I recovered from the initial shock and surprise, I bent back over the rail with a purpose. Now I really wanted that squid. It was still there, in the same spot, looking at me with the same glint of amusement in its eye.

I could swear it winked at me. I don't know if a squid can wink, but it sure felt like this one did. It let go of the boat and the hook, and in a flash of color it was gone.

Kenny came back and saw how I looked and asked what happened. I said, "I guess I was just set up and played by a clever squid."

Within an hour, I was dry, and my shirt was blue again. Vanishing ink must be another trick that squid had. I can only imagine the story it told to its friends. In another life, I would like to have been friends with that squid.

The next time I got one, I was ready. We took it home to eat after seeing how beautifully white the meat was. Kenny and I both found out that not all squid are good for food. Some people liked them and others, like myself, found them virtually in-edible. I sold some to my local market and half of it came back. Some people came back in looking for more, and others returned it saying it was horrible.

Even the Dungeness crab, known for eating anything, would not go into my traps baited with Diablo Rojo. Other fishermen thought they were the best crab bait ever found. One more conundrum for the record book.

The meat is pure white with a clear membrane that runs through it, making each bite a little chewier than a market squid, and market squid are chewy enough. This particular squid uses ammonium chloride to maintain neutral buoyancy at any depth. The market squid uses a different chemical for the same purpose.

The first hint of an ammonia taste at the back of my throat was not what I had expected. Once that taste was there, I could taste nothing else.

The nice browned steak of "cabaloni" I had been looking at on my plate was now suspicious. Had we not cleaned the squid soon enough? Was it my fault somehow that this beautiful meat was so bad?

Kenny had had a similar reaction to his first Humboldt squid. He had consulted his dad after dinner and found out we had prepared it incorrectly. What we needed to do was slice it really thin to cut the meat away from the membrane, then dip the strips in flour, then egg, then in cracker crumbs, then deep fry it and serve with tartar sauce. This was much better, but a pair of shoelaces cooked this way might be good too. Personally, once I tasted the ammonia, I could never get past the idea that it was still there. Some people think the Humboldt squid is fabulous eating, and sperm whales probably find them quite good as well, but I will never bring one home again.

Each year the squid became more common. They had become my new nemesis. I had fished these same waters for thirty years and had never even heard of a Humboldt squid. Starting in 1998, there were squid around during the winter months. The water is warmer in the winter along the California coast, because the wind shifts and the upwelling slows down. We thought that, as the water cooled in the spring, the Humboldt squid would go away, but every year there were more squid. By the year 2006, there was not a day of fishing that did not include dealing with these troublesome and feisty new creatures. They take the fish off my lines, hold on to a hook and swim backwards, making the job of getting my gear back in the boat dangerous and time consuming. There is not much I like about them, other than the fact that I respect them very much and would like to know more about their worldview.

I tried different markets to sell the ones we caught, but nobody really wanted them. They would pay me for the fish and take the squid on consignment. If they sold them in Chinatown, then they would pay me after they had been paid. These kinds of deals never work out well for the fishermen. In all my years as a fisherman, I do not think I have ever been paid for any of the various oddities I have brought in. Fishermen are at a disadvantage when it comes to marketing their product and all buyers know it. Fish do not improve with age. The concept of "buy low and sell high" may have been perfected in the fish buying business. C.O.D. is by far the best way to get money for fish.

The Humboldt squid had found paradise in California's northern waters. They were willing to put up with the cold water to enjoy the richest hunting grounds they had ever seen.

Eventually the ocean returned to its old self again, and the water cooled off. However, the squid had found Cordell Bank, and they were reluctant to leave. Special spots are not found every day, and the squid knew a good thing when they saw it. I don't think they will ever leave.

It is believed that all squid live a very short and active life. Scientists think they can accurately age a squid by counting the rings of growth on the thin, fingernail-like material found inside its body called the denticle. Common and current belief ages the squid at three to four years for their entire life expectancy.

There is growing concern that a large population of Humboldt squid feeding on the Cordell Bank could diminish the rockfish populations that are starting to rebuild. These squid eat everything from fish on down to the tiny krill and everything in-between. They can actually grow to be nine feet long and weigh ninety pounds.

Squid are thought to have one of the highest metabolisms of any marine organism. They can consume twenty percent of their body weight in a single day. It is thought that squid do not sleep. They hunt and eat twenty-four hours a day every day. The squid may be the animal that actually survives mankind's world domination. They spend most of their time in places where we can't bother them.

The arrival of these squid at a new spot could suggest a shift in the entire balance of the ocean ecosystem. As mankind overfishs parts of the ocean, and removes his preferred species, other "less desirable" creatures probably will replace them. Nature tends to fill empty spaces.

Most squid have ammonium chloride in their bodies. Ammonia is lighter than water, and the squid probably uses it to maintain neutral buoyancy at all depths. The ammonia also makes the meat taste like ammonia.

Any species that remains distasteful to mankind has a distinct evolutionary advantage over all competitors. On the East Coast, where the famous cod fishery has collapsed, there is concern that the dogfish has filled the niche the cod once enjoyed. The dog fish is not one of those fish that inspire great cooks. The meat has a slight grayish tinge, and, like all sharks, it tastes like the urea that runs through its veins.

Are we overfishing the oceans, or are we providing another avenue for evolution to weave its web? Who can say they see the pathway life on earth will follow? Mankind has a heavy footprint. Perhaps the American Indians had it right when they believed we should step lightly on this planet.

****

In the old days, people made money from the oceans by extracting things from it. In our modern era, more money is extracted from the seas by non-extractive uses. Eco-tourism and scientific studies are the big money makers now. For every study that is completed, there is a recommendation for at least one more follow-up study. The future looks bright for the scientific community.

I don't know if it is ironic or paradoxical that fishing caused this sequence of events to unfold. Is it the odd irony that the end result will be a sea full of fish and no fishermen? Or will the scientists be right and there will be no fish, or fishermen, by

2050? The pendulum of life will make its swings and there is very little any of us can do about it.

There are some people who believe the oceans could use some time without fishermen, and they are right. The land could use some time without farmers, too. The air could use some time without cars and factories. The planet could use some time without people.

The demand for seafood is increasing, and the resources can't keep up. The fish farms claim to have the solution, but I fear it is another industrial solution that will be packed with consequences.

I thought somehow, in my naive, optimistic way, that the little guys would be allowed to stay, and the huge net boats that caused the collapse of the groundfish would finally have to go. I guess I was too trusting, too sure that all will come right in the end.

The word "sustainability" is used ubiquitously by both managers and environmental groups. The term has a nice ring to it, but what does it really mean? To me, it invokes a picture of a small town that can feed itself. A system of resource management that replenishes itself and has a fighting chance to "survive humanity."

Is it sustainable to consume other people's fish while our local stocks rebound? There should be ethical fishing guidelines, but what are they? There have been semi-effective international campaigns to slow the take of bluefin tuna, swordfish, and Chilean sea bass as these stocks fell to dangerous levels. All of this is re-active rather than pro-active management. It took hundreds of years to overfish the cod stocks on the east coast, and it took only ten years to overfish the Chilean sea bass in the southern oceans. Technology may save the world, but it has opened a door to fishing that was locked ten years ago. We now possess the capability to catch the last fish.

Every country in the world is constantly upgrading their fishing fleet. The efficiency model dictates that more fish be harvested in the least amount of time. The boats are getting more horsepower, the sonar is getting more accurate, and the demand for fish is increasing, while supplies decrease.

The piracy of Chilean sea bass is a good example. If a boat and its crew can stand the weather, it is possible to make a million dollars a month, or more, on a boat that cost three hundred thousand. Patrolling the southern oceans is virtually impossible, so the chance of being caught is low. Piracy lives on, and what was once Spanish gold coins, is now fish.

Read HOOKED...the last great piracy

The Cordell Bank is famous for its populations of "groundfish." This includes all the fish sold as red snapper or rock cod, the sole and flounders, and the black cod, also known as butterfish. It is a term the managers use to describe all the fish that associate with the bottom of the ocean. In the 1970s, two thousand tons of these groundfish were landed in the port of Bodega Bay, the closest harbor to the Cordell Bank.

In 1999, the federal government was forced to admit that several of these groundfish stocks were at a turning point. Population estimates showed that some species were at ten percent of their historic levels. This realization started the long and painful regulatory process of getting fishermen to stop fishing.

At the same time, in the same area, the crab fishery has had record seasons. Everything is interconnected. One theory for the abundance of crab was the idea that the groundfish consumed mass quantities of crab larva. As larval predation decreased, crab populations increased. Nobody can say with certainty that the crab benefited from the demise of the groundfish stocks, but it is reasonable to surmise that.

HUMPBACKS

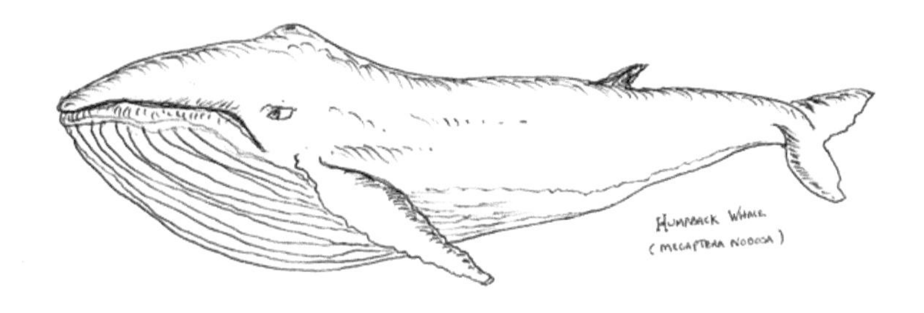

In the first great hunt for whales, in the nineteenth century, the humpback was not very popular. Whale oil was used to light the kitchens of the world and humpback oil smelled "fishy" when it burned. Sperm whale oil burned sweet, and barrels of it were worth much more.

Humpbacks were hunted extensively in the second great whale slaughter, at the beginning of the twentieth century. It all started with steam-powered ships and the ability to deploy a harpoon with a deck-mounted gun. Humpbacks are fast swimmers, but they were no match for the modern hunters. Whales were used for everything from women's clothing to cat food. Nothing was wasted in the modern whaling era. All the great whales were hunted by all the great nations around the globe.

Humpbacks are making an amazing comeback all along the California coast. They are, by far, the most common whale at the Cordell Bank. They never leave. For every one that travels on to Hawaii another one, or two, move in to take its place.

There are some animals that have adapted to living with mankind. The urban deer, the raccoon, the coyote and the mouse have all learned to co-exist with us on land.

In the ocean, it is the sea gull, the sea lion, and the humpback whale.

On land, we have the trickster animals. The mice that get in to places we constantly try to keep them out of. The dog and raccoons tipping over the trash can. On the boat, it is the same. The sea gull that steals the bait, even when you know it is there waiting. They know us better than we know ourselves.

The humpback whale is a trickster. It is not something I have that the whale wants; it is simply the fact that I am there at all that triggers the whale's curiosity and mischievous nature. More than any other whale, the humpback does things that can be for no purpose other than to enjoy itself, or satisfy its mischievous itch.

On TV ads, we see the humpback whale come out of the water, spin to the side, its flukes held wide, and come splashing down in an explosion of water. Why was the whale jumping in the first place? There is no reason to jump to catch the tiny organisms they feed on. There are no female whales nearby to impress with the height and grace of the leap. It takes a serious amount of energy to lift any whale out of the water, so why spend that energy?

Virtually all those whales we see on TV are humpbacks. Why they jump, or breach, is anybody's guess. Experts have theories I am sure.

I think they jump because it feels good. They are just burning up some of that crazy energy they were born with. Why do spinner dolphins spin when they jump? Just to be different? The idea that some other creature out there is having more fun than I am is disconcerting, but probably realistic. How much time in every day do we humans set aside for simply having fun? How much fun you had in your life could be the measure that really matters. That and how many people you helped.

Science probably does not consider the fun factor into many theories about animal behavior. Maybe it is because the scientists themselves are not seekers of fun. Having a good time is a reason to live, and humpbacks seem to know this simple fact.

The whale watching boats all love to find humpbacks, because the whales do not mind being around boats. If there is one humpback whale around, you can bet there are more not far away. They often feed like dolphins do, where they work as a team to herd small fish into a tight ball, and each whale has its place in the lineup.

It is virtually a fact that humpback whales can communicate with each other across the entire ocean. If they can, it is reasonable to assume that other whales can do this as well.

Observing whales from the deck of ship is nice and safe, but you feel distant, standing high above the water. As the boat gets smaller the whale gets bigger. If you really want to feel your experience of whale watching, I recommend viewing them in a tiny boat. A kayak is what the real whale watchers like to use. The farther out to sea you are the better. Distance from shore is another factor that can greatly enhance the size of the whale and your viewing experience.

Humpbacks are not big whales. Fifty feet is a big humpback. My boat is twenty-five feet long, so the average humpback I see is roughly twice my size. My boat is not big enough to feel comfortable amongst a pod of humpbacks.

My boat is about the size of boat they used in the first wave of hunting whales. I would never even consider trying to harpoon an animal that size from a boat this small. The hunter-fisherman instinct must have been much stronger in those men than it is in me.

I was fishing Cordell Bank one day when several humpbacks showed up and decided to hang out with us. They were not feeding on anything because they were so laid back. They were just swimming in slow circles around us with occasional breaks where they just stopped swimming and lay motionless a few feet under the surface, not moving at all.

My boat has what they call "low freeboard." This means that standing on the deck of the boat, your feet are only inches above sea level. It makes the boat more stable, but it puts you right there on the water. When one of those whales lifts its head out, ten feet away, and looks you in the eye, it is very up close and personal.

After an hour or so, the whales seemed to disappear, and we were not sorry to see them go. Any animal that is twice the size of your boat is intimidating. I climbed up on the back rail so I could sit down to bring in my line full of fish. This was a calm and balmy day. It was a lazy sort of day, and nothing was in a hurry. The water was very clear.

Groups of albatross had gathered around. The big black birds sat in groups of five or six. Each group of birds were all clacking beaks and making little noises, as if they were discussing and debating an issue. All around our boat were other birds, fulmars and gulls, relaxing in the calm, waiting for my fish to come to the surface.

It can take twenty minutes to bring in a line that has fifty fish on it. Where we currently fish, with the new laws, it is often a thousand feet deep. I settled in for the long haul and watched the birds discuss what was important in their world.

I don't know when I felt it, but the feeling was unmistakable. There was something watching me. It wasn't my friend Kenny, standing on the bow; he was looking off into the distance alone with his thoughts just like the birds.

It wasn't the albatross; they were busy with themselves and their various conversations carried on in their little groups. Not one of them was looking in my direction. And yet here was this feeling, intensely strong.

A few minutes of uneasiness passed, and then I happened to look down. It was as close to fainting as I have ever come. I almost fell off the back of the boat.

Looking down there was an eyeball, a huge, half open eye, looking up at me. I could see no ocean under the boat, it was all whale. One of those crazy humpbacks had been lying on its side, inches under the boat, watching me. One sudden movement by this inquisitive whale and we would be flipped over. I jumped off the rail and the whale ambled off, leaving me shaking and rattled.

Within minutes, the other whales had resumed their slow circling. The only difference was that now there were eight whales instead of two. This was uncommon but not unheard of, to have a small pod of whales circling a boat. If we had been on a bigger boat, and not thirty miles from shore, I could have relaxed and enjoyed the show. As it was, it looked like these humpbacks were having a fine time with their new toy. I was nervous.

The circles started to shrink. Each whale was trying to get the inside track and swim a tighter circle than the one before it. Now their tails were lifted high above the water in their efforts to turn the tighter turns. At one point, I looked up at Kenny standing on the bow, twenty feet away, and a whale's tail was eight feet above his head, the water dripping off the whale's tail was raining down on his head!

It was time to go. They were having fun, and I was terrified. Kenny and I put all the gear and fish away as fast as we could and slowly eased the boat out of the circle. I got us up to twenty miles an hour and drove for long enough to put those particular whales far behind us.

Was it intimidation tactics to get us to leave? Was it a fun loving group of humpbacks with nothing to do on a sunny afternoon? I felt no malice, but I did fear for my life. To this day I do not trust the trickster whale.

MAN AND THE WHALE

"There are old ones, and there are bold ones, but there are not many old bold ones." *Captain's Saying*

Drawings of whales have been dated as far back as 2200 B.C. Eskimos have been hunting them since 1500 B.C. In the twelfth century, the Basques started hunting whales from boats with harpoons. As whale populations decreased near shore, the Basques, and many other countries, moved to the offshore waters.

Tryworks (furnaces to get oil from blubber) were invented to render the oil at sea, and whalers ventured out farther and stayed longer to fill their holds with barrels of oil. Sperm whales were found to have superior oil in the 1700s, and the global effort to hunt these particular whales increased dramatically. The sperm whale became the whale that lit the world for several centuries. America replaced Norway as the top whaling nation, according to the book *The Whaling Question*, by Sidney Frost

By the end of the 1800s, petroleum replaced whale oil on the global market. Whale populations were down, and prices for whale products were down, so naturally the effort to hunt them went down as well. Whale populations got a brief break from humanity as we moved away from whale oil and moved on to fossil fuels.

Modern whaling really began in Norway when a guy named Svend Foyn created a cannon fired harpoon that could be fired from the bow of a steam-powered vessel in 1868. By 1872, this method had been fine-tuned to explode the tip of the harpoon three seconds after it hit a whale.

Fast swimming whales like the blue and fin and humpback whales had not been hunted in the first whaling efforts. With steam power and harpoons that flew far and exploded on contact, any and all whales were fair game. By 1913, the global whaling fleet was harvesting close to 20,000 whales a year. These harvest numbers are close to what they were in the peak years of the first whaling effort.

The next big improvement in whaling efficiency was the "stern ramp" in the 1930s. Whales had always been tied to the side of the ship as they were being cut into manageable pieces. The stern ramp allowed the crew to pull the entire carcass up over the back of the boat and onto the deck. By 1930, forty-five thousand whales were harvested every year.

Quotas and size limits were debated extensively. Just like the rockfish stocks at the Cordell Bank, the biggest quotas were eventually given to the countries, like Norway and America, that had harvested the most whales. World War II slowed the whaling effort substantially, but it came back with renewed interest and capability. Technology developed for the war was now available to the fishermen.

The International Whaling Commission was formed and they developed something called "the Blue Whale Unit" so they could fairly distribute the new quotas. One blue whale was worth two fin whales, or, two and a half humpbacks, or, five minke whales.

Australia, who was a top producing nation, generated the first scientific studies on whale populations. By 1966 nearly seventy thousand whales were being taken every year. The paradigm shift had started, but it took a push from Australia and a team of scientists from around the world to get it really moving.

The public became interested in whales. How intelligent is a whale? Do we feel right about killing intelligent beings? Do we have a right to deprive future generations their right to see these creatures?

The scientists report came back with shocking news. The report stated that the taking of another whale, no matter what species, was scientifically indefensible.

The last whaling company in Australia told the government they were going to lose money in the next few years because there weren't enough whales.

In the 1970s, Australia, the U.S., Norway, and many other countries sold their quotas to Japan. The money they got was a kind of bailout for the overinvested whaling companies.

****

The relationship between man and whales is evolving in a new direction. New sonar technology developed to track submarines in deep canyons is so powerful it blows the eardrums out of dolphins and whales if they are close enough to the ship using it. Every country with a navy will have to have this technology. It will only get more powerful as time goes by.

The killing of these whales is one more form of discard. Gloria's Golden Rule is clearly broken when whales and dolphins die so we can locate another country's submarine.

Cargo ships have replaced sailing ships, and modern cargo ships make a lot of noise underwater. Modern shipping has thousand-foot-long ships that travel at twenty miles an hour. When one of these ships hit a whale, even the mighty blue whale, that whale probably will die. The ship will not even feel the impact.

Ship noise might be like static on the radio for them. It is probably extremely annoying. More and more ships every year, and they get faster and faster. A whale can hardly hear itself think these days.

Ship strikes and low-frequency sonar kill more whales than hunters do in these changing times. We are saving whales with one hand and destroying their lives, again, with the other. This is another dialectic we will not solve any time soon.

We now compete with whales for their food for the first time in history. Humans are finding many uses for krill these days. As whale populations, and mankind, increases, the pressures on these limited food sources increases, and the poor krill had better find someplace to hide. Huge factory ships now harvest thousands of tons a year of the tiny krill whales depend on.

We primarily harvest the krill to feed the growing number of fish farms springing up all over the globe. Another interesting oceanic irony emerges: the idea that fish farms were going to ease the pressures humanity exerts on the resources of the sea. As the first years of intensive fish farming pass into history it turns out they may be doing the opposite. Another fine example of good intentions producing unexpected results, in a world absolutely full of unintended consequences.

*****

Man is sending a very mixed message to the whale. Stories in the news seem to suggest that some of the whales and dolphins are not the happy creatures they once were. In 2007, an "enraged dolphin" terrorized the French Atlantic coast, attacking boats and knocking people into the sea. A large sperm whale is responsible for the sinking of a Japanese fishing boat in the Pacific and killing two of its crew. We do, after all, threaten their very existence. Do they know that we know we could kill them all?

Whales and dolphins have larger brains than humans. It is reasonable to assume they have concluded that we are the cause of many of their current problems.

There is only one part of all the world man has not touched. A mile or two down, beneath the surface of the sea, an area not unlike outer space, the deep ocean remains virtually unmolested.

I have little doubt that we will soon be extracting things from the deep oceans at an increased rate. New life forms will emerge, and old theories will be replaced by new ones. Will we wake a sleeping giant? Is there a world of unforeseen consequences waiting for us several miles beneath the surface of the sea?

THE EVOLUTION

"And God created whales" *Bible*

A whale is not a fish. They are warm blooded, air-breathing mammals. They have a lifespan similar to elephants and people. The whale had a very unique evolution. Most mammals came from the water and evolved into land animals. We found land to be more desirable than water, and we stayed on land.

Sixty million years ago, the whale's ancestors decided that the water offered more opportunity than land, and they moved back to the sea. It could have been the meteor strike that destroyed the dinosaurs that motivated whale's ancestors to evolve back into the ocean. We will never know.

One of the possible reasons for why whales have much larger brains than elephants and humans is that it takes more analytical capacity to understand the world acoustically than it does visually.

There are over eighty species of whales (cetaceans). These are divided into two suborders: the Mysticeti and the Odontoceti. The Mysticeti are the baleen whales. They spend their days filtering the sea. It is from this order of whales that we see the largest animal to ever live on earth. Of the ten "great whales," nine are Mysticeti.

Some scientists suggest that ninety percent of all life forms have yet to be discovered. Virtually all of these undiscovered life forms live in the deep ocean. I sometimes find myself hoping there are intelligent beings living down there that consciously choose to avoid contact with the human race. What better place to enjoy a peaceful life, void of human interaction?

The other family of whales is the toothed whales (Odontoceti). These whales developed in a more predatory direction. This family branch includes the dolphins, the porpoises, the killer whales, and the sperm whale.

The killer whale is actually the largest dolphin and is therefore a high-ranking member of this formidable family. People who study animal behavior believe that it takes more brain capacity to be a predator than it does to be a grazer. This, coupled with the complexities of acoustics, could explain why the sperm whales and the dolphins have the largest brain on earth and the most developed cerebral cortex of any animal.

If man is the apex of mammals on land, then I would say this family, the toothed whales, is the apex of mammals in the sea. At the head of the table sits the sperm whale. It has the largest brain, it has a superior attitude, and very few creatures alive today could challenge its superiority.

The sperm whale is one of very few animals that can survive a dive of over a mile down. A sperm whale was found tangled in a cable that was in over six thousand feet of water. The pressures encountered in thousands of feet of water are enormous. During a typical dive, the lungs of the sperm whale collapse and the heart rate slows down to one beat a minute. They utilize more of the oxygen they take in than the human body does. Their skin is deeply wrinkled, and they have a thick layer of blubber that may help them in the intense pressure and cold encountered on deep dives.

The sperm whale loves its squid. Squid are the lords of the deep ocean. If you want to eat a ton of squid a day, you must dive thousands of feet beneath the surface of the sea to find them.

These whales developed a hunting technique that is unique in all the animal kingdom. Nobody knows for sure how they catch the squid they eat. Nobody knows how they even locate the squid. Science has developed many good guesses, but we do not know very much that could be called a fact.

The head of a sperm whale is filled with fine oil they called spermaceti. Apparently it has the consistency of sperm, and that is how the whale that lit the world got its name.

Experts all agree the whales use sonar, and they think the oil in the head can direct the sonar. They also think the oil might be used to concentrate the sonar beam to use as a weapon to stun the squid. Most of the squid found in the belly of a sperm whale are swallowed whole. This leads experts to believe the squid were stunned prior to consumption.

Squid don't show up very well on any sonar equipment I ever used. Squid are almost entirely soft tissue. They have no bones. Sonar requires a "return" from the pulse of sound, and a soft organism doesn't give a good return. We know the whales eat a ton of squid a day, but we can only guess at how.

If whales can pass on information to their offspring like other mammals, there is little doubt that small boats, about the size of mine, are regarded as very dangerous. Are small boats a target for retaliation? In the old days of whaling it was the small boats that threw the harpoons and did the killing. Can a whale hold a grudge?

THE OTHER INTELLIGENCE

"People need sea monsters."

The kraken was a sea monster that was part of everyday life four hundred years ago. Most of the drawings show a squid-like creature climbing up the side of a sailing ship holding some unfortunate crewman in one of its eight arms and threatening to grab other men with the other seven arms. The tentacles are wrapped around masts and down open hatches, searching independently for prey.

There are hundreds of years of accumulated stories about huge squid attacking ships. Can they all be untrue?

I caught a big octopus one day in a crab pot. It was bright orange, and it weighed over one hundred pounds. We poured it out on the deck of my small boat, and we tried to get it into a fish box. Kenny had one tentacle and I had another. The other six tentacles were exploring the boat, from bow to stern. We couldn't move it an inch.

After ten minutes of wrangling with this octopus, we gave up and just sat down waiting for it to climb out of the boat. It wasn't interested in climbing out. It was checking out the motors and steering cables with a few tentacles and poking around the bow with some others. In the middle was the big orange head with those big black eyes watching us, wondering who we were.

I got an idea. I had heard that octopuses like dark damp places. I opened the back hatch that exposes the belly of the boat. I have a bilge pump in there so I can get any water out that might have found its way in. It is a dark and damp hole that we use as a fish box on sunny days.

Within minutes, one tentacle found the hole and went in. Quickly three others had found it. The head of the octopus was bigger than the hole for the hatch, but that isn't a problem for an octopus. These creatures can fit into some very tight places.

It was like watching a magic trick. How do they do it? He had tentacles as big around as my upper arm. Its head was huge, and his or her body was the color of caution tape. In a very smooth slow motion, the octopus was in the box.

I closed the hatch and that was that. Man outsmarts another beast. I was going to let it go, but it had been eating five big crabs all at once. Most of my pots in this area had been empty, and now I knew why. Octopuses love crab.

When we got in, I made some phone calls and nobody wanted to buy it. They might take it on consignment. I thought people wanted octopus, but apparently, they only like the small ones.

I found an Italian guy who ran a seafood restaurant who didn't want to buy it but he would pickle it, and we would split it. He said it was a lot of work but it was excellent, so we did our deal and he took the one-hundred-pound slimy glob away in his truck. What had once been an incredible creature had turned into a formless gray tangle covered in suction cups.

As the weeks went by, I felt worse and worse about killing that octopus. I kept remembering the time when it was a stalemate. I remembered it looking at me with those big eyes waiting for me to try something. I resolved that if I ever got another one, I would let it go. I would take it for ride far from my crab pots and let it go around a reef where it could find a new life.

A month later I found four quart jars of pickled octopus in the front seat of my truck when I came in from fishing. I was amazed that I actually got some, but was that really all I got? Four quart jars of pure white discs floating in a clear liquid with various spices. One would think that a one-hundred-pound octopus would yield more.

I gave Kenny his two jars and put mine in the fridge. When I tried it, I was not expecting to like it. I expected pickled octopus to be chewy and fishy.

It was small white discs, like slices of bread and butter pickles. I tried a tiny disc, and I couldn't taste it. It simply melted away and was gone, so I tried another piece. At first the flavor is the pickling tartness and then there was the faintest hint of the sea. I ate another piece and another.

I began to think I might have just discovered the finest seafood I had ever tasted. I had to stop eating it and save some for my friends who needed to try this. Only one and a half jars were left.

Months later I bumped into the Italian guy again. He is a hard guy to find. I thanked him for the jars and hinted that more would be greatly appreciated. He assured me that what I got was half of what there had been. I asked how he had prepared it. He told me it was a very old family recipe that involved a pressure cooker.

How long do you cook it? How did you clean and prepare it? What were those spices you used? Do you want to do it again if I get another one? No, he didn't want to do it again. He couldn't say what spices he used or how long he cooked it. All I got for my probing and praise was a grunt.

I haven't kept a single octopus since then. I just let them go and feel good about it. In the bigger picture, I feel guilty taking a life that is so intelligent and interesting, so I don't do it anymore, even if it is the finest seafood I ever tasted.

The scientists who are looking for the giant squid should consider these aspects of morality. What will happen when we do figure them out? The squid will be exploited and another great mystery will vanish.

Shakespeare might be right again about this "wanting being greater than the having" concept. We all need some mystery in our lives.

Why not just leave it alone? They have eluded you for all this time, so why not just let it go and stop hunting for them? You can still be a scientific expert on giant squid without killing them in the name of science.

*****

Squid have good eyes. Could a huge squid climb up on a motionless ship and grab crew members eight at a time? I don't see why not.

We search the heavens to find other intelligent life when some of it may just lie under the surface of the sea. One of the leading scientific experts on the giant squid, Clyde Roper, in Richard Ellis's book "In Search of the Giant Squid," said that if he didn't know better, he would think these squid (architeuthis) were avoiding contact with people.

Is it because the squid live in an area where people can't easily go, or is it deductive reasoning and evasive maneuvering by the squid? Any contact between man and the giant squid will be disastrous for the squid. Perhaps the real sea monster is not the squid. Perhaps mankind is the monster.

An angry whale is one thing, but a pack of hungry giant squid has much greater potential for destruction. As man continues to deplete the seas, will the squid feel the pressure and begin to look for other food sources? Will the squid finally be forced to interact with us in the new world we have created for them? Is there a movie where hundreds of squid find a crowded beach in New England and grab swimmers eight at a time? I know there was a movie where a shark got swimmers one at a time on a crowded beach.

HOW TO GET STARTED

Common sense tells me that man's first contact with whales was when somebody found one washed up on a beach. Whatever led that person to cut into the dead whale hoping to find a use for it is what intrigues me.

I have walked by many dead whales washed up on beaches in various stages of decomposition. All of them were nasty. Obviously, they are huge. The possibility that there might be some edible part beneath the thick layer of skin and fat must have been compelling. I can just imagine the reaction when first man came into camp with a chunk of dead whale.

Maybe the discovery of whale oil came when the tribe threw the stinking blob he had brought home into the fire to get rid of it. The flames shot up and everybody was impressed. The skin and blubber of a whale will burn long and hot. It probably wasn't long before beached whales were a treasure.

Waiting for a dead whale to wash in while there were whales swimming by within plain sight must have been frustrating. In the days before humans had boats, there were probably many more whales swimming the seas near shore.

The next thing first man had to do was to invent a boat. I have been building and re-building boats for as long as I can remember. I think it started with floating sticks down gutters in the rain. Boats provided access to the sea and the fish. One successful fishing trip leads to another, and the boats eventually got better.

There is no such thing as the perfect boat. There are boats that are worse than others, but there isn't one that is better than all the rest. Every design has its inevitable flaw. Some may do well in a following sea, but they are unsafe going into the swell. For other boats, the opposite is true. Some are beautiful to look at and horrible to go out on.

I like boats that will not sink even if you fill them completely with water. I like the ones that have two of everything. I like boats with two motors, two radios, two fuel tanks, or two masts with two sails and two people on board. You can walk away from a car that breaks down, but not a boat.

Boat design has a long way to go. I would love to see what we come up with in the next hundred years. I like to think my little boat was way ahead of her time. I have filled it with water and still motored in. I have blown up an engine and still came in safely on the second motor. We got caught in fifty-mile-an-hour winds twenty miles from shore and lived to tell the tale.

She is a tough little boat, but there is no way I would ever consider harpooning a whale with it.

*****

If there is a universal law that all fishermen understand, it is that one big fish is better than a bunch of small ones. There are no fish bigger than a whale, so it was only natural that somebody eventually tried to catch one.

At certain times of year, some species of whales swim close to shore. Seeing them swim by, day after day, must have been very tempting.

The baleen whales, the ones that filter their food, are the more passive of the two families. They swim slowly most of the time and are much safer to approach in a boat.

The learning curve must have been a long and hazardous process. The idea of throwing a harpoon at the whale was obvious, but how to stay attached to the whale so it didn't just swim away with the harpoon was something else. Rope was not easy to make back then. Long pieces were even harder to produce and handle.

Hundreds of boats must have been flipped when the end of the rope came tight and the whale was still attached. An injured whale is going to be swimming hard.

Somehow the rewards must have justified the risks, because we continued to hunt whales. By the end of the 1600s, people were hunting whales on a global scale. Up to this point in history, nobody had ever dared to hunt a sperm whale.*

"Myself have agreed to try whether I can master and kill this spermaceti whale, for I could never hear of any of that sort that was killed by any man, such is his fierceness and swiftness."

Richard Stafford's letters from Bermuda, 1668.

The first boats to ever get up on "plane" must have been boats attached to a terrified whale. A boat on plane skims across the surface of the water as opposed to a "displacement" boat that plows through the water. Whalers called it the "Nantucket sleigh ride." What a rush it must have been to be towed across the ocean at speeds no boat had ever achieved.

To be involved in the actual hunt of any whale was an honor, and being a whaler was a respectable profession. They provided a service to mankind and they were proud of the service they provided. There is no prey any bigger for man to tackle.

The culture with the most spiritual connection to the whales is the Eskimo. Perhaps they were the first people to ever harvest a whale. Science told the Eskimos that whales only lived sixty years, and the Eskimos disagreed. Science told them how the whale's entire life cycle worked, and the Eskimos shook their heads.

A bowhead whale was killed by a tribe in 2006 that had a flint harpoon tip still embedded in its flesh. The harpoon tip and the whale were found to be over two hundred years old. Not all anecdotal information is wrong, and not all scientific information is correct. Will science ever learn the difference between theory and fact?

It wasn't until the middle of the seventeenth century that somebody did successfully hunt and kill a sperm whale. It was these first sperm whale fishermen that discovered the existence of the giant squid. They found pieces of them in the stomachs of the whales, and they saw the deep scars on their bodies. Herman Melville may have been the first writer to describe the squid through the eyes of Starbuck, in the book *Moby Dick*:

"In the distance, a great white mass lazily rose, and rising higher and higher, and disentangling itself from the azure, at last gleamed before our prow like a snow slide, new slid from the hills. Thus glistening for a moment, as slowly it subsided, and sank. Then once more arose, and silently gleamed. It seemed not a whale; and yet is this Moby Dick?"

In their search for the white whale, they had come across the only other creature more elusive than Moby Dick. From the description, I believe Melville himself saw a living giant squid.

The whaling fleet he was with in his youth had been fishing in a newly discovered area called the "offshore grounds." It was located one thousand miles west of the Galapagos Islands. This area is as far from shore as it is humanly possible to go. It is also the area where the sperm whale population chooses to live today.

Current population estimates suggest there are two million sperm whales. The majority of them live in this part of the southern Pacific Ocean. If the whales like it in these waters, then the squid must enjoy this area as well. As far from humanity as it is possible to get.

A really big sperm whale could yield up to fifty barrels of oil. Each barrel held 267 gallons. Oil wasn't thick and black and stinky like it is today. Whale oil was pure and sweet. This was the oil that lit every lantern in the civilized world. In the 1700s and 1800s, every streetlight and every kitchen light used whale oil.

The actual act of killing the whale was done in twenty-foot rowboats. The ships that carried these boats and their crew, and the barrels of oil, were eighty to one hundred feet in length and often stayed at sea for several years.

It is not a common sight, in the vast expanse of the sea, to see a whale. It is very rare to find whales in great numbers. To find a pod of whales that stay in one place long enough to allow the crew a chance to launch their twenty-foot-long rowboats and row out is rarer still. All these events need to line up in order to have a whale swim close enough to the hunter's boat to throw a harpoon into its back. I am not surprised that the average whaling voyage took years to complete.

Killing any animal should give the hunter pause. The taking of any life should make us reflect on our own mortality. I have found it much easier to take the life of a fish than to kill a bird or a seal. I can find no real rationality for this distinction, other than the fish is food and the seal was an accident.

I do not fully understand why I am reluctant to harvest intelligent life forms. Why is it easy to kill a fish for food and not an octopus? I don't think I would ever hunt a dolphin, even if I was hungry. But, I wonder…if all animals would be on the list if I were hungry enough. We take a life to give ourselves life.

There is no reason why whales shouldn't contemplate their own mortality and feel that they are a part of the bigger picture of eternity. Elephants demonstrate behavior toward their dead that suggests they have spent some time contemplating death.

This reflection on life, and where we pass to when we pass on, is not just for humans to think about. What about the whale or the squid? What goes on in the brain of an animal that lives a mile below the surface of the sea? We assume they live in total darkness, ignorant and spineless, but what do we really know about how the squid or the whale sees its world?

THE SQUID

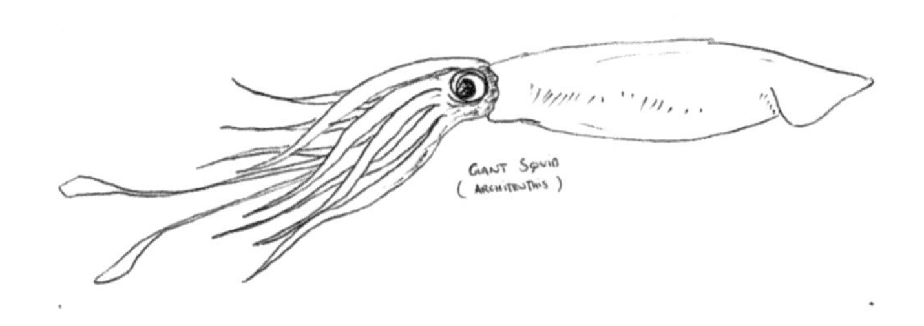

There are over seven hundred species of cephalopods. These include the octopuses, cuttlefishes, squids and chambered nautiluses. They are considered by many scientists to be the most evolved invertebrates. They have large brains. Many of them can control the pigment in their skin, allowing them to change color and texture in a flash.

Some captive octopuses have even been taught to do tricks like memorizing a maze. Some experts compare an octopus's intelligence to that of a typical house cat. I have had cats all my life, and I am still not sure who is the more intelligent, me or the cat.

The squid is a visual analyzer. A mile below the surface, there is no light. Why does the animal that has the biggest eyes our world has ever known need these huge eyes in complete darkness?

The squid use their eyes in a way that is a stretch to the human mind. Their eyes can create light at one moment and then receive the reflection from that light in the next. Like having a spotlight, turning it on and then off, they can use the total darkness to a great advantage.

Light speed is 186,000 miles per second and sound travels at 4,400 feet per second. The squid must process its return much faster than the whale.

I think I do need sea monsters to believe in. Somewhere in our psyche, there may be the hope, and the fear, that there is life on this planet that is smart and dangerous and elusive and we haven't seen it yet.

The giant squid is the ultimate lurker. It will see you long before you will see it. I am so glad that there is a creature like this, and at the same time, I hope I never see one from the deck of my little boat.

Is it a sign of intelligence for the squid to have avoided contact with humans? Or is it simply the fact that the squid live in an area that is difficult for humans to visit? Is it a conscious choice or pure luck that they have eluded mankind for hundreds of years?

HUNTING THE DEEP OCEAN

There are as many things we don't know about how the deep ocean works as there are stars in the night sky. Thanks to inventions like "critter cams" and G.P.S. tracking technology coupled with many hours at sea, there are some known facts.

Sperm whales can dive over a mile down. They can hold their breath for up to ninety minutes. Their heart rate slows down to one beat a minute on a deep dive. They swim at three knots (under four miles an hour) while hunting. Teams of scientists have successfully tagged and tracked the whales long enough to know this much about them.

Nobody knows how they catch so many squid. It takes the whale twenty minutes to get to the depth where the squid are and another twenty to get back to the surface. On a one-hour dive, this leaves only twenty minutes of actual hunting time if the squid are near the bottom.

Four miles an hour is slow. Squid, like the Humboldt squid that I saw, can swim twenty miles an hour and can turn on a dime. Squid can reverse their direction in a heartbeat. How does the whale catch any squid when they can out maneuver him, out swim him, and probably see him first?

Whales have small eyes and each eye sees a different world. A whale's head is so big it can't see past its nose. Their eyes have a very limited range of vision, being located where they are on the whale's body. It is safe to say that the whale is not a visual hunter.

This is where we step off into the world of speculation. Nobody really knows how sperm whales hunt so successfully. Nobody knows why sperm whales hunt squid rather than the thousands of other things they could be eating. The generally accepted theory is that the toothed whale family uses advanced echolocation to locate and somehow immobilize their prey.

Echolocation is sound bounced off an object. High and low frequency sound is sent out somehow from the whale, possibly using the oil in its head to concentrate the beam or broaden it, depending on how close the object is. If the sound beams hit something, it bounces off and returns. Nobody knows how much power a whale can generate or what frequencies it prefers.

It is the complicated interpretation of the returns that require a lot of brain capacity. The sound bouncing off the bottom of the ocean or off a mountain underwater is probably an easy and clear return, forming a good mental image. It is the differentiation between a squid and a fish or jellyfish at three hundred yards that would be much more difficult.

Man is a visual animal. We have a three-pound brain, and apparently most of us use only a small part of its potential. Sometimes I wonder if some of us use any of it at all.

A common dolphin weighing two hundred pounds has a four-pound brain. They turn off half their brain when they sleep. Dolphins must constantly keep surfacing to breathe so they can't completely relax and zone out. Humans might benefit from learning this trick.

Apparently, the light we see is actually reflected light. The light that bounces off the object we are looking at is what we see. Similar in many ways to echolocation, both are in response to the returning images.

The squid generates its own light from special light-producing cells called photophores. Little is known about how the system really works, but we know the light can be turned on and off by the squid. Other cells called photoreceptors receive the reflected light. The squid sends out a beam of light in the darkness of the deep ocean, and if it gets something back, it can decide to check it out or to swim for its life. The experts are convinced that the squid can determine the size, shape, and distance of an object from interpreting the returns of the reflected light. However, this is still a theory, not yet a proven fact.

I use echolocation on my boat to locate fish and "see" the bottom. I have one of the more expensive models of these "fish finders" because I fish in very deep water. The machine I use is a chromoscope. It is basically a high definition color TV with a lot of power, up to 3000 watts. I have had one of these fancy fish finders for twenty years, and I still am learning how to differentiate between one kind of fish and another. The echoes that return to the machine show different colors according to density. A small object will show up as a blue dot. An organism a little larger will mark green. The next size up will be yellow and on up the color spectrum to the largest objects that are a bright red. The actual bottom of the ocean, that is the most solid, marks as a reddish brown on the screen. The line of the bottom will be thin if it is a soft muddy consistency, and the line will be very thick if it is rock. This is a fabulous tool for finding fish, and it is mesmerizing to watch. I can see whales on it very well. They mark like a red worm on the screen.

An ideal mark on my machine, when I am looking for fish, is a red blob touching the bottom with a yellow haze above it. On top of the yellow haze, there must be a sprinkling of blue dots. Without the blue dots, there is a good chance there will be no fish biting.

I still don't know for sure if the blue dots are the fish or if the red is the fish. If I try a spot with only blue dots, it is usually a miss. Sometimes all red without the sprinkling of blue dots on top is good, but not consistently. If the red doesn't quite touch the bottom it is never very good. Some days there are marks everywhere, and some days we look and look for anything that remotely looks promising. I'm sure the whale's system is more advanced than mine.

Sperm whales do not use their teeth for hunting. We know this because when they cut them open and examine the stomach contents, it is obvious they swallow the squid whole. How does the whale catch a ton of fast moving squid every day and not bite them to catch them? The inside of the whale's mouth is an iridescent white. Do the squid just swim right up to the glowing white tunnel?

Squid are well armed. Some of them have cat like claws around every suction cup on every tentacle. They have powerful beaks. The tentacles alone can wrap and constrict. They can deploy a cloud of ink.

The most popular theory is that the whale locates a pod of squid with its echolocation and then blasts the entire pod with a concentrated and directed beam of sound. The whale then just swims around picking up the stunned squid. No biting or catching is required with this theory.

If that theory were true, then there would not be the deep scars so often found on a sperm whale's body. Some squid obviously battle it out with the whale. Certain squid may stun easier than others.

Science knows the whale eats its food whole because in the 1960s, when many countries were still hunting whales, the ships often carried scientists to collect data. Eight thousand squid beaks were found in the stomach of one sperm whale.

Sperm whales also eat fish. Salmon, rockfish and even skates have been found in the stomachs of these whales. The researchers also found rocks, sand, a glass fishing float, deep sea sponges, and a human boot. The preferred food is squid, but in a pinch the sperm whale apparently eats anything that looks edible.

On board one of the Russian whalers in 1971, a scientist noted that two of the whales they harvested were blind and several had their jaws broken. All these whales were full of squid just like the ones without these handicaps. They came to the conclusion that the whale doesn't need its eyes or its jaw full of teeth to hunt successfully.

Sound travels very well in water. I can't help but feel sorry for the whale that now has to sort out the differences between all the new sounds in the ocean. With constant ship noise, the other echolocation devices like my fish finder, the sonar, it is no wonder the sperm whale swims the seas with an attitude. I see why they might enjoy the spots that are far from human activity.

How far away can the squid see the whale? Is the range of vision different for different kinds of squid? Does the whale have limited range with its beam? Can the giant squid see the whale and stay out of range until the whale starts for the surface? Can the whale direct its beam backward to protect itself from behind?

Does the whale eat the giant squid, or does the squid eat the whale? Most squid swim in packs. Do giant squid swim in packs too? Could a whale defend itself against a group of thirty giant squid?

Here is a story published in the Marine Observer, London, 1998. This takes place in the Arabian Sea at night on some kind of cargo ship… "We were visited by a large school of giant squid—I think. They just rose out of the deep to look at us, about two hundred of them. There were some babies the size of a bucket, and adults, the biggest having bodies 3-4m long. We lowered the loading ramp to get a good look, and the captain's granddaughter took photographs—which probably didn't come out because of the very bright lights and the creatures being in shadow. The eyes were very large, bigger than a dinner plate, but the most remarkable thing was the color. The top of the head was red, like a Ferrari, and the tentacles were white covered with red spots which made them look pink. Where the red back joined the white area around the eyes, there was a pattern of interlocking spots. The crew tried to catch the babies but once hooked they broke free, and that individual could not be hooked again, which was interesting. They stayed for about an hour and a half, and then slowly sank from view. I mention this because I have heard on several occasions that no one has ever seen the giant squid` but I do not think this can be so… Has anyone else seen these creatures? It was interesting also because it is an area where there are female sperm whales."*

* Richard Ellis - Search for the Giant Squid

One solitary giant squid is one thing, and a school, or pod of two hundred of them, is an entirely different scenario. Would the mighty sperm whale stand a chance against this pack of two hundred hungry squid? The whale is on a time schedule, and the squid is not. At the end of a dive, the whale needs air, and this is when I would attack a whale if I were a squid. If we can just keep him from reaching the surface, he will weaken quickly.

If squid only live four or five years, how do they get enough food to grow to be fifty feet long? Eating a whale would help.

Squid have a system that literally grinds up the food they eat before it reaches their stomach. This makes it very hard to analyze the stomach contents. Nobody really knows what the squid are eating.

No scientists have ever seen a squid capture a whale, and they probably never will. Does this mean it never happens? If a tree falls in the forest, and nobody is there to hear it crash down, is there no sound?

THE WHALE BY THE TAIL

Theories are often regarded as fact if enough time passes and nobody challenges the accepted theory. One of these assumptions or theories is that the predator/prey relationship between sperm whales and giant squid goes one way and not the other.

What does this huge population of squid feed on? What does the small population of giant squid feed on? They must eat a lot of something to grow so large in such a short lifespan, if, in fact, the giant squid does have a short lifespan.

If humanity continues to deplete the seas, will these squid move into shallower water in search of another food source? I can easily imagine what would happen if a pack of twenty-foot-long squid descended on a popular swimming beach. Each squid could grab up to eight people at one time: a quick tentacle around the ankles and down you go. Twenty squid show up and fifty people vanish in several minutes of confusion. There would be no blood on the water, or any real sign that anything had happened. The squid could disappear like a dream and leave no trace.

****

In the 1960s, the hunting of whales was in full swing. The methods used for "harvesting" the whales had become much more modern and deadly. The harpoon was still the tool of choice, but the days of men in rowboats throwing the harpoons were long gone. The whale boat had evolved into a fast ship not unlike a "destroyer" used in World War II.

On the bow of these ships, there is a harpoon gun that fires a harpoon with an exploding head. They fire these harpoons with rope attached to them just like the first whalers did. You still need to hold on to what you hit.

The Russians and the Japanese and Americans collected all kinds of data about the whales they hunted. One little tidbit the researchers discovered was that the sperm whale doesn't catch many giant squid. Two percent of the squid beaks in their stomachs were from the true giant squid (Architeuthis).

Sperm whales may have a hard time getting close to the giant squid. The squid may know exactly where the whale is. I am just guessing about this theory, but I do know that light travels faster than sound. The squid hunts with light, and the whale hunts with sound. The squid will know more about the whale sooner, and this is an advantage all top predators wish they had.

If we were an intelligent group of squid trying to hunt a whale, we would wait in the distance, out of range of the whale's offense until the whale finishes its hunting and starts for the surface. This is the whale's weakest time, and any predator worth its salt would know this about its adversary.

All we need to do is come up behind the whale on its way up and grab on to its tail and swim (or pulse) backward until the whale runs out of air and energy. The whale by the tail is the safest possible spot to grab on. If it shakes one of us off, someone else will grab on. We can do this.

Elephant seals can dive several thousand feet down in search of their favorite food. Huge sharks swim at these depths as well. It only stands to reason that a squid the size of

Architeuthis would feed on creatures like elephant seals and sharks and whales rather than thousands of small fish. If they are only four years old and they do eat twenty percent of their body weight a day, what are they eating to grow so big so quickly?

Great minds knew the world was flat, so we believed. What do we believe today that will seem ridiculous tomorrow? The squid/whale relationship might be due for some new revelations. My father once told me that "Intelligence is the ability to change your mind."

After I was attacked by what we called the ragged tailed sperm whale off Cordell Bank, I became fascinated by the idea that the animal with the largest brain this planet has ever known hunted the most elusive animal man has ever encountered. Half of half of this deranged whale's huge tail had been chewed off by something. There was so much missing from the tail that it could no longer swim in a straight line. My science friends think it was killer whales that chewed its tale. It could have been killer whales, but this was a full grown male sperm whale, and killer whales don't usually take on animals like this. I like to think it was a pack of squid.

THE SILENT SEAS

I like the stories. I like the idea that there are sea monsters. I think the sperm whale qualifies as a first-rate sea monster, but the giant squid is more otherworldly. It flashes light, and it has giant eyes. It is the mythical creature come to life.

Here is a story that was printed in the London Times on July 4th, 1874. I found it in Richard Ellis's fabulous book, *In Search of The Giant Squid*. There are hundreds of stories, and I am sure that the very best stories have never been told. Nobody lived to tell those tales.

"We had left Colombo on the steamer Strathowen, had rounded Galle, and were well in the bay, with our course laid for Madras, Steaming over a calm and tranquil sea. About an hour before sunset on the 10th of May we saw on our starboard beam and about two miles off a small schooner lying becalmed. There was nothing in her appearance or position to excite remark, but as we came up with her I lazily examined her with my binoculars, and then noticed between us, but nearer her, a long, low, swelling lying on the sea, which, from its colour and shape, I took to be a bank of seaweed. As I watched, the mass, hitherto at rest on the quiet sea, was set in motion. It struck the schooner, which visibly reeled, and then righted. Immediately afterwards, the masts swayed sideways, and with my glass I could clearly discern the enormous mass and the hull of the schooner coalescing—I can think of no other term. Judging from their exclamations, the other gazers must have witnessed the same appearance. Almost immediately after the collision and coalescence the schooners masts swayed toward us, lower and lower; the vessel was on her beam ends, lay there a few seconds, and disappeared, the masts righting as she sank, and the main exhibiting a reversed ensign struggling towards its peak. A cry of horror came from the lookers-on, and as if by instinct, our ships head was at once turned towards the scene, which was now marked by the forms of those battling for life—the sole survivors of the pretty little schooner which only twenty minutes before floated bravely on the smooth sea. As soon as the poor fellows were able to tell their story they astounded us with the assertion that their vessel had been submerged by a giant cuttlefish or calamari, the animal which, in a smaller form, attracts as much attention in the Brighton Aquarium as the octopus. Each narrator had his version of the story, but in the main all narratives tallied so remarkably as to leave no doubt of the fact As soon as he was at leisure, I prevailed upon the skipper to give me his written account of the disaster, and I now have much pleasure in sending you a copy of his narrative:

"I was lately the skipper of the PEARL schooner, 150 tons, as tight a little craft as ever sailed the seas, with a crew of six men. We were bound from Mauritius for Rangoon in ballast to return with paddy, and had put in at Galle for water. Three days out, we fell becalmed in the bay (lat.8`50'N,long 85`o5'E). On the tenth of May, about 5 P.M.—Eight bells I know had gone—We sighted a two masted screw on our port quarter, about five or six miles off, very soon after, as we lay motionless, a great mass rose slowly out of the sea about half a mile off on our starboard side, and remained spread out, as it were, and stationary; it looked like the back of a huge whale, but it sloped less, and was of a brownish colour; even at that distance it seemed much longer than our craft, and it seemed to be basking in the sun. "What's that?" I sung out to the mate. "Bless if I knows; barring it's size and colour, and shape, it might be a whale" replies Tom Scott; "and it ain't the serpent," said one of the crew, "for he's too round for that 'ere critter." I went into the cabin for my rifel, and I was preparing to fire, Bill Darling, a Nawfoundlander, came on deck, and, looking at the monster, exclaimed, putting up his hand, "Have a care master; that 'ere is a squid, and will capsize us if you hurt him." Smiling at the idea, I let fly and hit him, and with that he shook; there was a great ripple all round him, and he began to move. "Out with all your axes and knives," shouted Bill, " and cut any part of him that comes aboard; look alive, and Lord help us!" Not aware of the danger, and never having seen or heard of such a monster, I gave no orders, and it was no use touching the helm or ropes to get out of the way. By this time three of the crew, Bill included, had found axes, and one a rusty cutlass, and all were looking over the ships side at the advancing monster. We could now see a huge oblong mass moving by jerks just under the surface of the water, and an enormous train following; the oblong body was at least half the size of our vessel in length and just as thick; the wake or train might have been 100 feet long. In the time I have taken to write this the brute struck us, and the ship quivered under the thud; in another moment, monstrous arms like trees seized the vessel and she heeled over; in another second the monster was aboard, squeezed in between the two masts, Bill screaming" Slash for your lives," but all our slashing was to no avail, for the brute, holding on by its arms, slipped his vast body overboard, and pulled the vessel down with him on her beam-ends; we were thrown into the water at once, and just as I went over I caught sight of one of the crew, either Bill or Tom Fielding, squashed up between the masts and one of these awful arms, for a few seconds our ship lay on her beam-ends, then filled and went down; another of the crew must have been sucked down, for you only picked up five; the rest you know. I can't tell who ran up the ensign.

"James Floyd, late master, schooner PEARL."

There have been over 150 confirmed specimens of the giant squid that washed in all over the globe. The biggest was fifty-seven feet and it was an Archeteuthis, but there are other squids that get big, New Zealand and the Newfoundland area being some of the hot spots for finding them beached. Four-hundred-pound squid have been found whole in the bellies of sperm whales.

Some of the stories describe squid that were nearly two hundred feet long, twice the size of the biggest blue whale. The Newfoundlander in the story knew what it was, and he also knew not to piss it off by shooting at it. I sympathize with the skipper of that schooner, because I made the same mistake he did. I didn't actually shoot at the whale; I shot behind it to scare it away. The result was similar. Neither I nor the skipper of that schooner considered the possibility of angering the animal. The unanticipated consequences of our actions could have killed us both.

THE RAGGED TAILED WHALE

Once again, I am thirty miles out off the California coast fishing with my friend Kenny. We have fished together for close to thirty years, and he is still a pleasure to fish with. Kenny is the only person I know who consistently out-fishes me. If I catch thirty fish on my line, Kenny will probably have fifty. Every once in a while, our roles reverse for a few days, and I think I am learning and catching up. Thirty years is a long time, and I am still learning.

It is late September, and we are out where the whales play. Late fall is the best time for viewing the open ocean whales in Northern California and the Cordell Bank. We were going to a spot west of the bank called "the football." It is a ninety-nine-fathom-high spot—or 594 feet—that looks like a football on the chart.

I remember expecting to see whales and even looking forward to it. Kenny was with me when we saw the first sperm whale many years ago. The passing of time had softened the edges of that memory.

I had seen one other sperm whale in the years between the first and the third. The second one was gun-metal gray, and it did the same thing the first one had done. It lined up and came right at us. I did the same thing I did the first time and put the boat in gear and got out of its way. Thankfully, it just passed under the boat, and we never saw it again. This whale had been at the football. The second one wasn't as big as the white one, but it was still in the fifty foot class. After it passed by, I remember thinking that this must be normal sperm whale behavior, and I should expect it from the next one.

When we got to the football, the wind was up a bit more than we had hoped for, and the seas were choppy. We got out of the comfort of the tiny cabin and out into the wind to put our gear in the water and look around.

The fish finder lit up. There were literally acres of some kind of life under our boat but the fish were not cooperating. I suspected that all the marks on the fish finder were not fish. It was probably something like krill, the tiny shrimp-like organisms that birds and fish and whales all feed on. Hundreds of thousands of pounds of krill were concentrated around the football. This is another spot that everything likes to visit.

All in all, it was a rather uncomfortable, unproductive and uneventful day. The fall is like that often. It is a transition time on the ocean, just like it is on land. The Cordell Bank area fills with all kinds of life. There are more albatross, more whales, more feed, and the fish stop biting for some unknown reason

Around three o'clock, Kenny spotted a whale. "Did you see that whale?" he said. "Its tail came clear out of the water." Not me, I didn't see it, I even recall saying to myself that with my luck, the way it has been lately, we wouldn't see another one for the rest of the day.

Then we both saw it, and it was not far away: a dark gray whale with a raggedy tail. I had never seen a whale with its tail all chewed apart. Half of half its tail was gone. I remember wondering how a whale could get its tail chewed off like that.

Again, the whale surfaced. It had a narrow head that was so characteristic of a sperm whale. And, just like the last two sperm whales I saw, this one had altered its course and was coming right at us. I don't know what it is about sperm whales, but they make me extra nervous.

No other species of whale had ever come this close to hitting my boat, by accident or on purpose. Thousands of whales had passed nearby over the years, and only the sperm whale had taken an aggressive interest in our little boat. I still can't help wondering if these whales were told what little boats did to them in the past, and now they are not going to put up with us any longer.

Both of the previous whales had spotted us from quite a ways out. Both times I had had to start my motors, bang on the sides of the boat, wait for them to get close and then bump the boat into gear and move out of their way at the last minute. Both times this strategy had worked, and after they had passed under us, we never saw either of them again. I was ready for this one.

The first one, the white whale, was the biggest. If some of the blue whales we had seen were over eighty feet, and I am sure they were, then the white whale had to be close to sixty feet long. Sperm whales get big.

Our third sperm whale, that day's whale, was slightly smaller than the other two had been. It was probably less than fifty feet long. It had deep scars all over its head and body, and it was now only a few hundred feet away. The tail looked more and more like something chewed on it. This was the first moment I thought squid might attack whales. The scars all over this animal's body were everywhere. Deep gashes all over its head and back and down near its eyes. This guy had been in some serious battles. He had not escaped serious injury. Could it be that some giant squid gnawed on it in a failed attempt to catch this whale? Or was it a successful escape from some killer whales that left this whale looking the way it did?

The whale was not acting like a normal whale. For one thing, it couldn't seem to swim in a straight line. Every time it came up, it seemed slightly off center. It appeared to be swimming in a huge lazy circle, twisting as it dove. A dog with rabies walks the way this whale swam. It was possible that this whale was sick, or mentally impaired. It was also possible that the whale was desperate and hungry because of its ailments and its inability to swim or dive properly.

Just to be safe, I decided to start the motors. This way I could at least move away if this mad dog of a whale blundered too close to us. The decision to be careful was the right one, because a moment later the enormous back of the whale with the raggedy tail was fifty feet away and coming right at us!

I put the boat in gear and moved forward and out of its path. We watched it fade into the depths behind us and wondered about this curious whale. "At least that episode with another one of those sperm whales is over," we said. Nowhere in my mind did I think I would ever see that whale again. That was an animal with a history. He was obviously a rogue male that had fought and survived some serious battles. Can you imagine the stories that whale could tell? The aging bull still hanging on to life.

I turned the motors off, and once again we were drifting along fishing. It felt like I had ten or fifteen fish on my line, and Kenny probably has a few more. It takes at least fifteen minutes to retrieve a line from six hundred feet, so we started the lines up and began to talk about maybe trying one more spot before going home.

The weather was too rough to be called very nice. The twenty-knot breeze out of the northwest is cold for a September day. The white caps and the waves passing constantly under us made life on a little boat like mine uncomfortable. The boat was tough, and it could probably handle rougher weather than I could.

I had my line half way up when I saw that same raggedy tail again. It was a hundred yards away, but it looked like it might be turning in a slow circle to come back in our direction. "Great," I say to Kenny, "did you see that too?" I got this eerie feeling that this was the beginning, rather than the end, of our visit with this whale.

The motors were still off, and we continued to reel in our lines. There was a definite apprehension in the air. I happened to glance up to the bow of the boat where Kenny was sitting, reeling in his load of fish. He was looking in my direction, but he was looking past me. His eyes were open very wide, and his mouth was open, but there was no sound coming out. Kenny lifted his arm to point at the same moment I heard it behind me. It was the sound of moving water. Something really big was moving water out of its way. The whale was back, and it was ten feet from the stern of the boat where I sat!

Out of nowhere and with no warning, the whale had circled back around and lined up on us from beneath the surface. It had probably echolocated us the same way it echolocates its prey.

This was not a good situation. That was way too close for comfort, and thank God the whale couldn't swim straight, or we would have been upside down. My boat may be a good sea boat for its size, but it will tip over if a fifty-foot whale comes up under it.

I am not sure I have ever felt quite like that before. Was this whale really after us, or was it just overly curious? Maybe it was looking for a mate, I don't know. To be on the better side of caution, I started the motors again before we continued to reel in those fish that were still on our lines.

The weather being what it was and this weird whale had Kenny and I talking about just getting these lines in and going home. It was going to be over an hour to get back, and the fish weren't really biting. I still did not feel that we were in any real danger. The whole event seemed like some kind of fluke we were lucky enough be part of. The rigs we used were all hand tied, and we get attached to them. Each hook had been tied with colored feathers and flashy material to make them sparkle in the water. Kenny tied his rigs, and I tied mine. We put a lot of time into those rigs, and the thought of losing them was tragic.

If I had known then what I know now, we would have cut them and run. There were fish on the lines. We don't want to just abandon those fish and break Gloria's Golden Rule. Bringing the fish up and onto our boat is certain death for the fish, no matter what the whale does. As fishermen, the thought of cutting lines and running away from a whale seems ridiculous.

Once again, being careful pays off. Can you ever be too careful? Here came our whale again. This time it was off the bow of the boat. I jumped down and put the boat in reverse moving out of its path once again. This time, we got an excellent view of the deep scaring along its back. There was no doubt now that this was not just a coincidence. The whale was not going away. It had a purpose, and we were at the center.

Maybe I was too worried about the money. To cut our lines would cost hundreds of dollars in gear and fish. Kenny was of the same mind as I am: just get the lines on the boat and get out of there. I was limited in my ability to maneuver with the gear out, and I certainly couldn't jump to twenty miles an hour. Speed is my little boat's most valuable asset.

Many of the mistakes we make in our lives begin with a quick flash of a good idea. Only after we act, what seemed like a good idea at the time turns out to have been really stupid. When we reflect back, it is obvious where the mistake came from, but at that moment, the quick good plan prevails and the mistake is made.

My plan was to scare away a sperm whale. The whale had made too many attempts at ramming our boat, and I came up with the quick solution. I decided to try some persuasion. I have never liked guns. I get nervous every time I load one. The only reason I even had one on the boat was to scare away sharks and sea lions. It works pretty well on those creatures, so why not with a whale?

Many of my fishing buddies had heckled me over the years for not carrying a gun on the boat. I finally bought one. It was a stainless steel shotgun they called a halibut gun. I assume it was for shooting big halibut prior to bringing them onto the boat. I used light gauge bird shot for the biggest splash. My friends insisted I needed the gun for safety, but somehow the whole idea of guns and safety touches me as a contradiction, a "make war so we can have peace" kind of contradiction

So now, here I am, putting a shell in my shotgun to make a loud noise and a big splash to scare away a persistent sperm whale. The whole event sounds absurd, but that is what I did.

Looking back, after considerable reflection, it was a stupid idea. In recent years, the sharks and sea lions had been so bad I had bought the shotgun. Never in my wildest dreams had I imagined I would be using the gun to scare a whale away from my boat. If it had worked, it would have been a good idea.

The whale surfaced again twenty feet off the stern, and *boom;* the shotgun did its job, making a tremendous splash ten feet from the whale's back. The whale got the message. The boil it left behind was a clear indication I had impressed the whale. "That will do it," I said to myself.

Somewhere in my subconscious mind, I must have known it wouldn't work. Instead of reeling in the lines, Kenny and I just watched the water. I was in the cabin with the engines running, and Kenny was standing by the window. It was very quiet.

I didn't get a scared whale; I got a pissed off one. Instead of leaving us alone, it intensified its assault against us. In fact, the whale's next move was to try to bite our boat in half.

This was the one time in the thirty years Kenny and I have fished together when I saw him truly upset. We had been scanning the surface for any sign of the whale. Time went by with nothing but wind on the water. For some reason, Kenny looked down instead of out. Our faces were only a few feet apart when he looked at me with terror in his eye. "Get us outta here," he squeaked. As he gripped the edge of the window preparing for impact, I looked down into the clear water and could see the whale coming up, its mouth wide open.

I put the boat in gear and slid forward just in time. The whale's body came half way out of the water twenty feet behind the engines. The splash was the size of a house. These whales have long jaws and huge teeth. We would not have survived his attack if we hadn't moved.

Scare away a sperm whale? What was I thinking? Do they even know what fear is? I do not think a shark or a sperm whale knows the meaning or feeling of fear, and why should they? Why would any of the very top predators have the need for fear? It is the emotion that keeps the lower animals, like us, alive. Fear is of little use to the unchallenged master of any given domain.

I can understand these master predators feeling anger, or annoyance, or curiosity, but the fear was for me that day, not the whale. I think it is a good survival technique to be a little fearful in any situation involving big animals. Know their patterns and look for the signs, but pay attention to the fear factor in your soul, and listen to that inner voice that can alert you to something your conscious mind might miss.

I was afraid to stop the boat. A moving target is harder to line up on, especially if you can't swim in a straight line like this whale. But, I have to say, for a whale that gave the appearance of being physically handicapped, it certainly had been accurate in its assault.

We motored around in zig zags for some time still dragging the fishing lines. I still did not want to cut the lines. Five minutes went by and no whale. We stopped the boat and started reeling in as fast as we could.

Finally, we saw the ragged tail again. Kenny and I were clearly elated and relieved to see it was several hundred yards away. The wind and current were both going the same direction that day, and our adversary was both down wind and down current from us. This was the first good thing that had happened to us in the last forty-five minutes.

At last, we could get the lines and the fish on the boat. All things considered, we both agreed that leaving this entire area and going home sounded really good. As anticipated, each line had ten or fifteen fish. Instead of taking the fish off the hooks and stacking the rigs like we normally do, we just pulled all the hooks and fish into a big pile on the deck. The quicker, the more nimble, the better. I knew my boat was faster than any whale.

The wind was stronger now. We had no idea if the fishing was good or bad. The idea of running to another spot nearby was not appealing. At this point, both of us had had enough fishing. I know I didn't care to see another sperm whale for as long as I lived.

Just as we were getting underway, we saw it again, that raggedy tail high in the air. The whale was not downwind from us anymore. It was upwind and only one hundred yards away, coming straight for us again.

Things were a little different. For the first time, I felt confident that the whale would not get anywhere near our boat again. With less than five hundred pounds of fish below decks, my twin one-hundred-horsepower engines would jump the boat up to twenty miles an hour very quickly. I seriously doubted that this whale could catch us at that speed.

I was feeling much more in control and relieved we were prepared to bid farewell to the whole business. I set the course for home and tried to relax and shake off the emotions. Looking out the open cabin door we saw it again, for the last time. It was well behind us now, but this time it was not alone. Two new sperm whales had joined our ragged tailed whale, and they all were headed our way. The two new whales were smaller and appeared to be normal, healthy whales. They were the usual dark grey color, and they seemed to be swimming straight. Maybe they had come to help their buddy out of a difficult situation. Was it possible that the first whale actually called in for reinforcements?

This was enough for me. I gave the wheel a turn, gave the motors lots of gas, and away we went. I never even looked back.

On the ride in, I don't believe either of us spoke a single word for the first half hour. It was just too much all at once.

Kenny and I had seen a lot of strange things over the years, but in my mind, this was the creepiest event we had ever shared.

We had had some life threatening days. There was engine trouble, thirty miles out, with the sun going down. There was the freighter we could hear but could not see because the fog was so thick. The propeller of the freighter churned the water very close, and the fog was so thick it was impossible to tell if the ship was outside us or inside. There were radical changes in weather, and there was the giant surf. All those things seem to pale in the shadow of the whale.

To this day, I don't know if the whale with the raggedy tail was sick, hungry, horny, or just had an itch on its back it couldn't scratch. But I do know that if it had done what it wanted to do to my little boat, I wouldn't be here to tell about it.

The next morning, lying in bed, I kept thinking about the whale and wondering if it would do the same thing to another small boat. I thought about calling the Coast Guard to report our experience and alert them to the possible danger to other vessels. At first, I was embarrassed to call and admit I had been scared by a whale. Then, after talking to my wife about the whole sequence of events, I looked at it from another angle. What if I read in the paper about another boat being attacked off Cordell Bank? What if this other boat sank and people died? How would you feel about not alerting the Coast Guard then?

I called the Bodega Bay Coast Guard station. I reported where we were and all that had happened. My fears were confirmed when the officer did not take me seriously. He sounded bored and I am sure he did not "alert" anybody. I was just another fisherman with a story to tell. I felt stupid for having called.

The skipper on the schooner who shot at the squid and I who shot to scare a whale have something in common. Neither of us was thinking clearly. We both thought of the quick solution without considering the possible consequences of our actions.

WHAT IS INTELLIGENCE?

The ability to learn or understand from experience. The ability to acquire and retain knowledge. To use reason to solve a problem. A degree of keenness of mind, cleverness or shrewdness. To anticipate an action, and what the results of that action might be. These are a few of the many definitions that attempt to define intelligence.

One of the ways man tries to separate himself from all other animals boils down to the idea that we have convinced ourselves that we are smarter than the rest of the creatures on earth. It is interesting that we are our own judge and jury on this issue. We can find no other impartial entity to judge for us. By default, we win the "smartest animal on the planet" award every year.

Is it a coincidence that the sperm whale population consumes the same amount of seafood every year as the entire world's population of fishermen? You know the world's fishermen are trying as hard as they can to catch what they catch.

The whales are not competing with us….yet. This is a good thing for the whales.

The next generations of humanity would probably appreciate it if we didn't keep eliminating species. I have hope that we will do the right thing.

My dad once told me, "Hope...don't leave home without it."

How smart is it to create technology that could destroy the whale's, or our own, ability to live on this planet? I fear we have the invincible attitude of teenagers when it comes to technology. All of us feel it will save us, in the nick of time, from what we are doing to ourselves and our planet.

Global warming will be halted by the new thinking that is just around the corner. Cleaner energy and advanced technology may not save us from constantly growing global economies, unlimited population growth, and a planet that is staying the same size.

We created nuclear energy, and we do not understand the end game of this new technology. We have poured our sewage into virtually every river in the world, and the consequences are still not fully realized.

Every river makes its way to the sea. Can human activity upset the balance enough to inhibit the blooms of phytoplankton? Without the oxygen produced by the tiny one-celled plants in the sea, all of us will perish. Everything is interconnected. The overall health of our oceans is something we should pay closer attention to.

Perhaps the oceans are more sensitive than we think. How long can we use them as a giant garbage can and not pay the price?

THE SMARTEST BIRD

On a lighter note, I have observed a certain bird that clearly displayed deductive reasoning. There are clever birds and there are beautiful birds, but it is a rare bird that has both those qualities and the ability to reason out a problem.

I have gotten to know quite a few birds in my years around the water, and only one stands out as a thinker. Does this separate them from other birds? How far down the animal kingdom chain does the word "intelligence" apply? I think any animal that can solve a complex problem with deductive reasoning is, by our own definition, intelligent.

The albatross has had a place in history as a bird of "omen." There is a "sign" associated with every albatross sighting. They are protected by an un-written law that says "you will not harm the albatross in any way." If you do, it will be at your peril.

I don't know anything about all the myths, but they have become my favorite bird to spend a day with. They are a very social animal. They are one of the only polite birds I have ever encountered.

Albatross are huge, but they don't use their size to be bullies like the sea gull can be. They fly thousands of miles over open ocean skimming for...of all things, squid. With their wingtips inches above the water, they dip their beak just inches under the surface and pluck squid from the water as they fly. Apparently there is an abundant quantity of a smaller squid species that lives at the surface in the open ocean. You never see an albatross if you can see land.

They are avian surfers, using the energy of the waves to increase their speed and distance traveled. Being a surfer myself, I imagine these birds derive some fun out of riding those waves. It would be hard not to.

Two examples of "deductive reasoning" stick in my mind and make me smile.

The fish I catch in deep water will float to the surface if they come off the hook. They get the "bends" like human divers get when they come up too fast. All the birds know this simple fact, and they tend to accumulate around the boat as the day goes on. The first lines I bring in will have a "floater" or two and a passing bird will see it and come down for a bite to eat. One bird sitting on the water seems to attract another, and in several hours, it is not unusual to have fifty birds, representing five or ten different species, all waiting for the next lines to come up.

On one of these typical days, there were several fish on the surface, each with its contingent of birds. All of a sudden, all the birds flushed. This means something scared them and they all took to the sky. All except the albatross. One minute there were fifty birds around our boat, and then it was down to a dozen albatross, all in a tight group, all focused on something under the surface that I couldn't see.

The thick dark shadow of an adult white shark was just visible below the birds. The shark was interested in the same floating fish these birds were eating. There was only one bright red fish still floating on the deep blue sea.

The shark's mouth is on the underside of its head. This meant that it would have to roll on its side to eat something floating on the surface. The albatross seemed to know this simple fact. The birds formed a line downwind from the fish, and as the shark made its approach, they were ready.

As soon as the shark rolled on its side, the birds started pecking at its eye, pulling on its gills, grabbing the pectoral fin, generally heckling the shark to distract it. To our amazement, it worked, and the shark missed the fish!

Sharks of this size (twelve to fourteen feet) need some time to turn around for another try, and the albatross took full advantage of this fact as well; eating as much as they could before the next pass from the shark. It took five tries for the shark to finally prevail.

On another day, I was fishing alone far out to sea. I was towing a line with sixty hooks dragging behind the boat. The hooks, with the bright feathers tied to them, must have looked like tiny shrimp skipping along the surface to a bird flying above the moving line.

Albatross don't usually make a mistake and get too close to the hooks, but on this day, one did. It must have flown down too close and then tried to pull up and got the tip of its big foot caught on a hook. The poor bird was getting dragged backward across the water behind the boat, and I knew nothing about it. I was looking ahead to see where I was going, not looking back.

I was motoring along, in my tiny cabin, when I heard an albatross squawking very near my head. These birds are normally quiet birds, they don't squawk very often. I turned around to look, and there was an albatross flying ten feet from the cabin door yelling at me.

I remember looking at the bird and saying out loud, "What is your problem?"

The albatross kept flying in closer and seemed quite upset. Then I looked back farther, and I saw his buddy getting towed backward by the tip of one foot. It had dipped down to inspect one of my pretty flies and got itself hooked in the soft webbing on its foot. The bird looked ridiculous skipping along behind the boat.

I stopped and quickly hand-lined all the hooks in to get to the bird. It calmly let me unhook its foot while its friend looked on from above. In a minute, all was good, and the two of them flew off together.

How did the second bird figure out that I was the only way to solve his friend's problem? The hooked bird was a hundred feet behind the boat. The problem was the hook, but the solution to the problem was sitting in a cabin on a boat. The solution to its friend's problem was looking the wrong way.

To help his friend, he had to get my attention. He flew up so close to the cabin door that I could hear his cry over the noise of the motors running. And it worked!

These birds displayed courage, reasoning, and team work, and are like no other. They rarely encounter a shark in their everyday lives, and yet they handled this one skillfully.

The albatross is rarely seen from shore. Perhaps this too is a sign of deductive reasoning and intelligence. Just like the sperm whale, the albatross knows that land means people, and people mean trouble. Even I can see that simple fact. Long live the albatross!

SELLING GLOOM AND DOOM

I think the ocean off the West Coast of the United States is healthy. It goes through warm water events and cold water regimes with grace and style. Population densities for various species fluctuate, but no life is static. I believe the oceans are resilient. I hope humanity gains the knowledge required to fully respect and appreciate the role the oceans continue to play in our lives.

There is a trend I see in our media and among the scientific community. They like to tell the tale of gloom and doom: "The world's oceans are dying," "By the year 2050 there will be no fish left in the sea." The birds are disappearing; the krill populations are half of their historic levels; seventy percent of the world's fisheries have collapsed. All the news about the oceans is depressing these days.

Some of the news is true. There are many places where destruction of habitat will forever change an area. There are "dead zones" popping up in places that were once full of life. But there are good stories, too. Seals and sea lions have enjoyed a seventeen-percent rise in population for ten consecutive years. Whales like the humpback and the blue are having a population boom. These animals are at the top of the food chain. To have a spike in the population of a top predator says a lot about the health of the ocean. The seals and the whales are finding enough food to eat.

The species that mankind has preferred over the years are in decline, but other life forms have taken their place.

I think there is more money generated by studying the ocean than there is in extracting things from it. Up until twenty years ago, people made money from the ocean by harvesting something. The tides of change have swept the fishermen from the sea and replaced them with research vessels. Unfortunately, bad news generates more study dollars than good news does.

Sustainability is the big word in our culture today. It is about time we take a serious look at what is and is not sustainable. Man can create a model of what a sustainable fishery could look like, but the variables undermine the model. We have only been keeping records for several hundred years, and that is a very short time in the larger picture of life. The idea that we can see patterns or understand the variables is just another example of our arrogance.

Some things are obviously apparent. If we as a species apply all our technology to the catching of any one species, we can eliminate that species. This is the power of mankind, and we would be wise to see it for what it is. The power is both gift and curse. Learning to know ourselves may be the biggest challenge facing mankind.

The American Indian had the idea of living as a part of the ecosystem, in harmony and with beauty. There is our hope and our sustainability in a nice package. Once you see the beauty, it is difficult to do things that might destroy or alter the harmony that generates the beauty. Appreciate and admire the fish you catch, and you are one step closer to a sustainable fishery.

THE GREAT WHITE DILEMMA

"The past is gone and the future is uncertain"

When a marine organism suffers a severe decline in population in the United States, there are laws set up to protect and preserve the creature in question. Any animal that is shown to be at or below ten percent of its historic or "virgin" population will fall under the protection of these laws.*

This concept is sound, but there are some interesting questions that arise in any human attempt to "manage" an ecosystem. Even in today's world of intense data collection, there are inaccuracies built in to the collection system.

Fisheries data are a perfect example. As a licensed fisherman, I am required to fill out a landing receipt for all the species of fish I land on a given day. On this receipt are boxes to fill in on where the fish were caught and where they were landed. The landing receipt data are used to "manage" the fisheries. The paperwork I fill out is the only way the government can keep track of where I am fishing and how much I catch.

What are the chances that fishermen fill out these records accurately? Why would any fisherman tell anybody where the fish are? One hundred years of inaccurate information carefully analyzed by top scientists produces vast amounts of useless information. However, it is still the "best information available."

This imperfect information is also influenced by human nature. All of us have an inclination to promote our own ideas, and scientists are still human and do the things humans do.

I call it "cherry picker science." In the vast array of data, you pick the stuff that gets you to where you want to go and discard the stuff that doesn't fit. It is surely not "scientific," but it is the way it is.

The great white shark is a working model of how this kind of "management approach" can create a serious dilemma.

White sharks were protected, years ago, when the "experts" estimated the entire West Coast population, from Alaska to the Mexican border, to be two hundred fifty animals. The white shark was immediately put on the endangered species list.

A few years later, there seems to have been a population boom. Beaches were being closed. People were being "sampled" by curious sharks, and eaten by hungry ones. I personally saw five white sharks in the month of July. How many are really living off the coast?

I have lived in Bolinas for fifty-two years. I have been running a boat out of Bolinas for forty years. It was a rare thing to see one white shark in a year of fishing. Many years went by without seeing one. I saw seven last year and five this year so far, and I don't fish as much as I once did.

What was the "virgin" population of these sharks? What are the unintended consequences of a population surge? Beach closures are more frequent now than ever before. Is there a shark season, or have they "discovered" the beautiful West Coast and its abundant seal and sea lion populations?

The seals are also protected and doing well. The shark and the seal are like the lynx and the white rabbit. The predators are probably having more babies, just like the seals did when they were no longer hunted.

A healthy ecosystem has room for all the creatures, large and small. The trouble seems to come when people step in and select some favored animals for protection and lose sight of the balance.

What, if anything, can we do about a booming white shark population? What will it mean to local businesses if beach closures become more frequent? I was surfing in Bolinas this week when someone I was surfing with saw a large white shark breach (jump) just outside where we were waiting for waves. We all went in as quick we could. Is surfing going to get too dangerous to enjoy? The experts assure me that the sharks do not prefer surfers. They know the difference between a surfer and a seal.

John McOscar, the white shark expert from Steinhart Aquarium, asked me how many times I thought a white shark had swam by me while I was surfing, and I didn't see it. He knew I had surfed in some spots where these sharks like to be. We were at a town meeting about two shark attacks in Stinson Beach that occurred in August. I had suggested "culling out" that shark with a gillnet.

John's point was that "most" white sharks know the difference, and why would I want to "cull out" any shark that was behaving itself? There is no guarantee I would catch "the" shark that bit the surfers. It is a good point, and the vote was against the gillnet.

The white shark is one of the most awesome creatures I have ever seen. They have every right to flourish in this abundant ocean we share with them. How the sharing will work out is the great white dilemma.

The science people demonize the fishermen, and the fishermen demonize the scientists. Environmental groups fight for what they perceive as the right path, and harvesters fight for the right to harvest the various resources the ocean has to offer. The past is gone, and the future is uncertain. Nobody has "the answer" to the real question: "How much can the ocean withstand and remain healthy?"

Humanity has been pilfering the seas for much longer than there have been record keepers. It is evident from the fish bones left in old European dump sites that humanity shifted from freshwater fish to saltwater fish around 1100 A.D. From these same bones, it is also evident that the fish were much larger back then. The lakes and rivers were probably being overharvested eight hundred years ago. By the eighteenth century, some researchers think we had scraped every inch of the bottom of the entire North Sea with trawls towed behind sailing schooners.

Science abhors all anecdotal information, anecdotal being anything seen by someone other than a "qualified" scientist. All the records of historic population estimates on whales and fish populations came from the whaling vessels and the fishing vessels that were hunting them. There were no scientific teams on the boats in the eighteenth century. Therefore, all the estimates on historic population numbers were derived from interpreting anecdotal information. What do you call a situation like that? Is that a true conundrum?

All our ocean managers use the term "best available information" when determining the status of the species of concern. Even if the data are shown to be inaccurate, it is still the best information available. A "fact" is even more elusive. Good data is very difficult to obtain on any marine organism, and the difficulty increases as the water gets deeper. How do you count fish that live six hundred feet beneath the surface? How do you count whales when all you see is the mist of their blows far out to sea? How could you possibly get an accurate count on a white shark population?

In reality, the whole process is guesswork. No matter how carefully we analyze incomplete information, the conclusions drawn from incomplete or inaccurate information will be both incomplete and inaccurate. The management councils and the science teams do not like it, but this is the reality.

Fishermen are the ones who complain the most about all the guesswork and all the "studies" that are being well funded. Each new study asks more questions than it answers. The conclusion of each new study is that another study is needed. Another study is needed to fill the gaps the last one revealed. The fishermen are left standing on the land looking out to sea while the science team heads out in their state-of-the-art research vessel.

There is no question about needing good science to help us understand the many complexities of the marine environment. The more we know, the more we will need to know. Fishermen all around the world are worried about survival. All the small town ports along both coasts of this nation are losing their fishermen. Just like in nature, when something leaves, something else takes its place. The small town ports will slowly vanish, and corporate-owned factory ships will replace them. The waterfront where there were once fish docks will fill with condos and restaurants. The weaker species moves aside for the stronger one.

My little port is a fine example of how the current system is playing out. In the 1980s, there were twenty-two boats making a living in my town. At the beginning of 2008, there were five. Today there are three fishermen who are just plain stubborn.

Every species of fish has its own special permit, and every permit has its own special price and renewal fee. This year it cost me two thousand dollars to renew the three permits I qualified for. Every year the fees for these permits go up, and the amount of fish they allow you to catch goes down. How long will it be until the law of economics prevails, and the last small time fisherman walks away from his boat?

If they do all walk away, and a few years later we decide that we actually want a few back, how do you do it? None of the old guys will have passed on the important stuff to the new younger guys. It will be interesting to see how it all unfolds. Perhaps another study could shed some light.

California recently passed a law that produced a network of marine protected areas. The idea is that an area with no take of any species will produce "emanation zones." Big fish will produce more offspring that will emanate out from these protected areas into the areas where fishing is allowed. I like the concept. If we could leave something, anything, that is still pristine for future generations to enjoy, they will look more kindly upon our graves.

THE DOLPHIN DAY

"If I was ever to be re-incarnated, and I could choose what animal I would become, I would be a dolphin."

Dolphins like boats. Their favorite thing to do seems to be play. They live the good life. It is more important to enjoy life at this moment than at any other moment in time, and the dolphins seem to have embraced this philosophy wholeheartedly.

Dolphins love to jump out of the water. But why? I can think of no practical reason for the jumping; it certainly does not help hunting in any way. It must just be fun. Launching yourself out of the water, using the energy of the ocean swells to assist, must be a thrill they enjoy every day. Surfing is as close as humans will ever get to this feeling of unity with the ocean and playing with its power. I know from personal experience that surfing waves can brighten any day. The albatross surf on the wing, humans surf on a board, and dolphins surf a la natural. Great minds think alike.

The bow wake of a boat traveling the perfect speed, ten or twelve knots, is another thing dolphins can't resist. As the boat slows down to five knots, the dolphins get bored and swim away. If the boat speeds up to twenty knots, the dolphins race along with it for a minute or so and then fade away. They probably tire quickly swimming that fast. If a pod of dolphins comes along when I am running offshore at twenty knots, I often slow down to match their favorite speed. They would stay with you all day long at ten knots.

Not all dolphins are alike. Some only know one speed. The Pacific white-sided dolphin, Lagenorhynchus obliquidens, common around the Cordell Bank, never slows down. They remind me of some people I know who only know two speeds when they drive their cars, full throttle or stopped. I have never seen a Pacific white-sided swimming lazily on the surface enjoying the day.

The white-sided dolphin has a similar color pattern to the killer whale, black on top and white on their sides. Killer whales, on the other hand, do take time out to relax. They are the largest dolphins, and they are wise to the ways of the world.

Apparently, dolphins do sleep. I always wondered how and when they make time for it. There is the problem of breathing. How do you stay above the waves and breathe when you are asleep? It turns out that dolphins rest half their brain at a time. One half sleeps, and the other half swims and breathes. I wonder if I do this too on some level. I know that half my brain must not be working sometimes, judging by some of the decisions I have made over the years. As Ambrose Bierce once said, "Brain: the apparatus with which we think we think."

The Pacific common dolphin, Delphinus delphis, has the classic dolphin gray-on-gray stripes running down its body. It is an entirely different creature than the white-sided. These dolphins seem to put relaxation as a top priority. On the days when these dolphins are around, they just swim in small groups, circling slowly around the boat as we drift, in a lazy sort of way, not really paying attention to us, just hanging out. It was with these dolphins that I had my first little conversation.

I never see the white-sided dolphins mingle with the commons. Apparently, segregation is alive and well in the world of dolphins. I have never seen them hassle each other, but I have heard they do. I have never seen them hunting or swimming together.

I don't remember ever seeing any mixed pods of dolphins. Three or four different species of dolphins might be in the same general area, but they keep to their own kind as a general rule. They might not speak the same language.

It was a very calm day, and I remember there were ten or fifteen of these common dolphins that had followed us around from spot to spot for several hours. The fish were biting well, and we were bringing up lines with sixty bright red fish on the hooks every fifteen or twenty minutes. This had been going on for over an hour, and the dolphins had watched us catch over a thousand pounds of fish in that time.

I was sitting on the back rail of the boat, reeling in another full line, when I heard a voice inside my head ask a question. At the very same moment, there were several dolphins swimming very close, and I was sure it was a question from one of them.

"Why are you catching more fish than you can eat?" was the clear, precise question. There was no tone of disapproval or judgment; it was just a simple curiosity.

It is a good question. Humans do have a tendency to take more than they need. I have even asked this question to myself a time or two. The Cherokee Indians called it "the way." Never take more than you need, and never take the best. If you leave the biggest fish, or the healthiest deer, there will always be healthy fish and deer for you in the future. It is "the way" it is, and nobody can change the rules of nature, no matter how important you think you are.

I tried to explain: this is how our system, the human system, worked. I trade the fish for money, and I then use the money to buy the other things I need.

I felt kind of stupid when I listened to myself try to justify my way of life. I need to make money so I can buy more stuff. I need the stuff so I can support my family and come back out and catch more fish. I catch more than I can eat again so I can get even more money. What a wonderful web I have woven for myself.

There was a sense of acknowledgement, if not understanding, from the dolphins. Maybe there was even a touch of sympathy, but I am just guessing. I quickly explained that I thought their system was much cleaner. There is no accumulation of stuff, and you never take more than you need. I told them I envied the simplicity and purity of their way of life. To swim the oceans of the world and have no burdens was an advancement over the human condition, in my opinion.

"Oh no," the dolphins said. "You have it all wrong. There are times when we swim for weeks without finding any food. You don't know where to swim to find anything to eat, and the ocean is like a lifeless zone with no way out."

Apparently, they are confronted with that horrible choice between going ahead or turning around. Who will decide?

I had never thought about it that way before, but it does make sense. There must be vast areas of the ocean that have little in the way of food for a dolphin. I know from my own fishing that there are times when it feels like there are no fish in the sea.

Can you imagine how that must feel? The utter desperation of not knowing where to go to find food? The ocean is more like a vast barren desert; everywhere you look, it looks the same. Water everywhere. At times, there is life everywhere you look, miles and miles of fish everywhere. At other times, it is the opposite scenario. I don't know why, but I guess I thought dolphins had figured out how to be in the right place at the right time, all the time. Dolphins are more vulnerable to the whims of nature than we are.

I said, or thought, in response, "Even still, if I were ever to be reincarnated, I would choose your life, a dolphin's life, over another human life."

And as clearly as any voice I have ever heard, they said, in mild surprise, "Oh, you can't choose? We can!"

Our conversation was over as quickly as it had started, and I wondered where it all came from. I had never thought of the dilemma facing a dolphin when they swim for days without finding food.

They would like to see an ocean that has life everywhere. Dead zones, now ever present in this new world, are a dolphin's worst nightmare. That and the new sonar technology the navies of the world are using.

The idea that dolphins can choose what they will be in the next life is a new one for me. I am happy for them. I hope it is true. They seemed very surprised that I couldn't choose.

The idea that we might eventually be able to choose what we will become on our next visit to this world is fun. I find it very refreshing, and it makes me happy just thinking about it. As a kid, I think I wished to come back as a tiger. It was a wishing situation as opposed to a conscious choice.

When there is a question that has no clear answer—like "Where do we go when we die?"—we can choose the most pessimistic or the most optimistic options. The arguments are strong on both sides.

In the face of the unknown, is the gloomy option the one to live with? In the spirit of having a bit of fun while we spend this short time here, I think the theory that makes you smile is the one to believe in.

I must say a "thank you" to the dolphins for taking the time to talk with me. They broadened my perspective on the ocean, and on life, without a single spoken word.

THE PARADIGM SHIFT

With a fifty year "re-building" plan in place for the Cordell Bank, it does not look like there will be any more whale stories, or fish tales, to be experienced, or told, by me.

I just saw my sixty-fifth birthday go by, and my body is not what it was. I don't hear as well, I don't see as well, and I wonder when I become a danger to myself operating a car or a small boat out in the big ocean.

When is it wise to quit? The ocean doesn't care one way or another, but I know it only takes one mistake to be your last.

A fifty-year moratorium on fishing makes my presence on opening day rather doubtful. I'll bet the fishing will be really good after the nice long break. Too bad I won't be around to see it.

There is the very real possibility that nobody will ever see it, because when our government takes something away, they rarely give it back.

Our fishery was simple. One fishing rod each, hooks with pretty feathers tied to them to imitate something a fish might like to eat, and a big fishing reel with lots of strong line on it. What really made our situation unique was a combination of location and technique. The location, as I have mentioned, was, and is, a very remarkable stretch of ocean: underwater islands next to deep canyons, right on the edge of the continental shelf. It has an ocean floor that drops from hundreds of feet deep to thousands in less than a mile.

The technique we used had us spending most of our time drifting without the sound of a motor. In the old days of sailing ships, all the boats were silent on the seas. In modern times, it is the rare boat that does not have and use a motor constantly.

Any animal is easier to approach if you are quiet. The reverse is also true. Our tiny boat, way out in the really big ocean, was very easy to locate and investigate. This is why I think we saw so many of the rarer creatures. We were quiet, small, still, and usually unnoticed.

The stories about sea monsters climbing on ships at night and eating everyone on board were common in all the ports around the globe two hundred years ago. "Ghost ships" had been found and towed in. The ship was still floating, but there was nobody onboard.

The truth is that I actually feel safer driving my boat thirty miles out to sea than I do driving my truck to get to the boat. The unpredictability of the ocean is no match for the unpredictability of man and his devices.

In the old days, I could fish anywhere for anything with any kind of net or hook. On this day in 2017, I can only fish in water deeper than a thousand feet. The laws regulating fishermen went from one extreme to the other. In thirty years, we went from having so few regulations we were allowed to overfish and deplete the stocks of fish to a time like today, where a guy in a twenty-foot boat needs to be watched by satellite as he fishes in super deep water for the one kind of fish he is allowed on a limited entry permit.

America has completed a paradigm shift. We went from being one of the top seafood producers to being one of the top protectors of the marine environment. The current RCA (rockfish conservation zone) that Cordell Bank lies within is the largest Marine Protected Area in the world.

Fishing may have been one of the first occupations that was "watched" by our government. For seventeen years I have been required to have, maintain, and pay for, a vessel monitoring system (VMS). It is a satellite tracking system, professionally installed on my tiny boat, that is, by law, required to be on twenty-four hours a day. It feels like we have been singled out, like we are on probation for the obvious crimes we all commit every day we go out. It is common knowledge that fishermen are all liars.

In addition to the VMS requirement, every permit holder is required to take a federal observer with them every day they fish. Every observer I have taken over the years has come down to the dock, taken one look at my homemade boat, and they have their doubts about going thirty miles out in this tiny boat. They check the flares and the survival suits and the date on the inflatable raft I must carry. They check and check and in the end, we go fishing.

It usually takes about half the day for them to start to relax. By the time we start putting fish on the boat, they have found a spot to sit out of the way and they are busy keeping records of how many hooks I use, what color the lines are that attach the hooks to the main line, what bait I use, where exactly I set the lines, and how many fish we get. Data collecting is hard work.

It is the ride home that puts the smile back on the observer's face. Most of the boats they go on are big and slow. A twenty-mile ride can be four hours, or more, on the average trawler.

If the swell is big, and the wind is light, I can make that twenty-mile trip in under an hour. We surf home. Surfing is fun in a boat that is designed to do it, and once they get to trust the boat, they relax and enjoy it.

In rough figures, I would guess it costs you, the tax payer, fifty thousand dollars a day to watch me fish. By the time the observer's reports make it through the scientific network of analysts and regulators, those data they collect are expensive.

I got a letter from NOAA one day ten years ago. When I opened it, and read it, I almost passed out. The letter stated that I had been one-quarter of a mile inside the restricted zone, and if I would send them a check for $35,780, this issue could be resolved. No warning, no explanation of how something changed. I had fished that exact spot for seven years with the VMS on the boat, and all of a sudden it was an illegal spot. I had an observer on the boat on the day in question.

For six long years I fought that ticket. My lawyer tried his best, but the government is hard to beat. The federal judge was hired, and paid, by NOAA. I ended up paying $21,000, not counting the lawyer.

My boat isn't worth $38,780.

A few years later I met the head of enforcement for NOAA. I asked him for my money back. He laughed and said there are no refunds. Later, as we sat at dinner together I asked him why I had received the ticket. He said, "Because there are so few of you left." I hadn't expected such an honest answer.

I think it was because I attended meetings and spoke out about the inequities and the eventual corporate ownership of our precious ocean resource.

If they ticket me for violation, it discredits my position.

Sadly, it worked and I do not go to council meetings anymore.

THE SON OF MOBY DICK

I finally saw a sperm whale that didn't care that I was there. I have seen six sperm whales over the years, and five of those required evasive maneuvers to avoid being rammed.

It was in thick black fog and a choppy sea. We couldn't see a quarter mile in any direction. There were no other boats on the radar when I scanned the sea for an eight-mile range. I could hear the whale when it surfaced for air, but I couldn't see it. I knew it wasn't a humpback, or a blue whale, because the sound of the blow was different. I hoped it wasn't a sperm whale.

The whale and I were both there for the same reason. We were competitors in a way, each of us after the same fish, working the same spot. We could hear its powerful spouts somewhere nearby, but we couldn't see it in the fog and rolling ten-foot swell. Hours and hours went by, and we never saw each other or got in each other's way.

We fished together, the mystery whale and our little boat, and as the hours passed and the fish started to fill the boxes, we still had not seen the whale we were sharing this spot with. The fishing was excellent and neither of us was going to leave.

When I finally did see the whale, it was going by so fast that all I could be sure of was that it was a sperm whale. The forward angle to the blow was unmistakable. The other obvious thing was that it was a big one. Sperm whales like black cod almost as much as they like squid, and we were both fishing in a big school of black cod.

I thought it might be wise to put the gear on the boat and call it a day. We had been fishing around this whale for hours without a problem, but I clearly remember the other sperm whales I had met.

The fish were biting well and, in another hour, we would probably have enough to fill our thousand pound quota. It would be a shame to leave such good fishing. So, we took a chance and stayed.

A half hour later, I got my only really good look at the whitest animal I have ever seen. The narrow head that is usually covered in scrapes and scars was smooth. His massive back was like polished white glass. He was surfing a swell heading in our direction, so I could see how wide he was in the middle. This whale had not lost a battle in its entire life. It was by far and away the most impressive animal I have ever seen.

Whiteness is a mark of something beyond all the edges that define an animal. We look around this world, and we can see how the tiger is great in the jungle. The most impressive tiger of all is the Bengal tiger, white with turquoise blue eyes. Bears are at the top of their world, and the pure white polar bear is near the top in that group of animals. The great white shark is only white on its belly, but if it were pure white it would be even scarier than it already is. White man is another very scary creature, and a true, ever-present sea monster.

For some unknown reason, I felt comfortable sharing a spot with this whale. As comfortable as I ever feel fishing around whales. It was an honor to see it, and if the whale could feel my thoughts, like the dolphins did, that is what it felt from me.

Moby Dick was a loner, a rogue who was feared by all who came in contact with him. He was the true free spirit that would take shit from nobody. If you wanted trouble, he had it for you, and if you wanted to pass unharmed, just sail on by.

I like to think that the same "unchallenged" attitude still exists in some sperm whales alive today. I hope the squid feel it too. I hope we leave them alone and let them dominate their domain for many years to come.

It turns out that there are, in fact, pure white sperm whales; I am not making them up. Scientists have seen and photographed them. You can see pictures of them on the internet. I like to think that I shared a day of good fishing with the great grandson of Moby Dick.